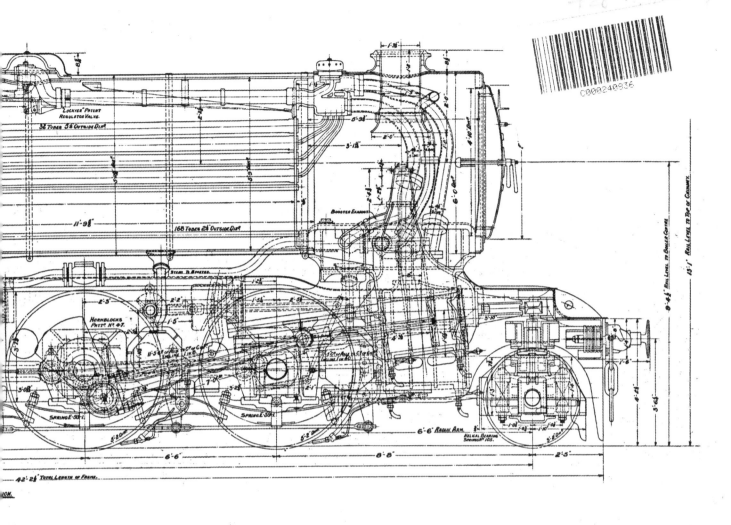

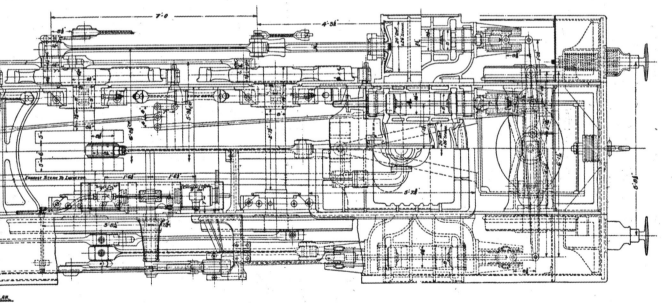

RAL ENGINE.

NDERS 20" x 26".

GRESLEY'S
CLASS P2 LOCOMOTIVES

GRESLEY'S
CLASS P2 LOCOMOTIVES

....

ANDREW HARDY

In association with the P2 Steam Locomotive Company

Ian Allan PUBLISHING

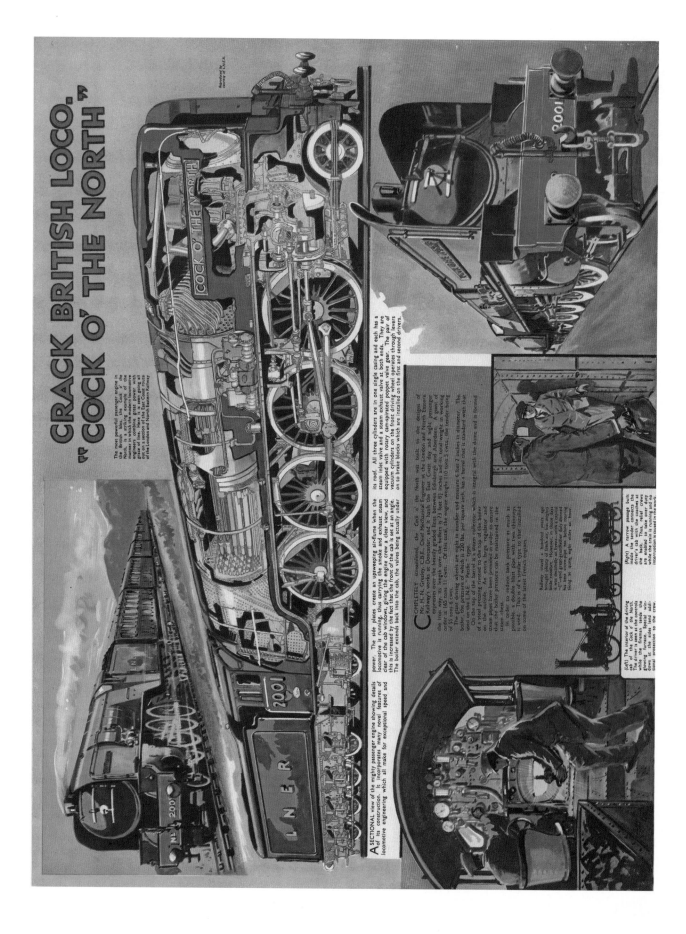

CRACK BRITISH LOCO. "COCK O' THE NORTH"

The most powerful passenger engine in the British Isles, the "Cock o' the North," is a striking example of the manner in which modern locomotive engineers combine great power with grace of line. Here it is seen going all out on a section of the East Coast Route of the London and North Eastern Railway.

A SECTIONAL view of the mighty passenger engine showing details of its construction. It incorporates many novel features of locomotive engineering which all make for exceptional speed and power. The side places create an upsweeping air-flume when the locomotive is running, thus carrying the smoke and exhaust steam clear of the cab windows, giving the engine crew a clear view, and this is increased by the fact that the front of the cab is set at an angle. The boiler extends back into the cab, the valves being actually under its roof. All three cylinders are in one single casing and each has a steam inlet valve and a steam exhaust valve, at both ends. They are equipped with rotary cam-operated poppet valve gear. The pairs of vacuum cylinders on the front driving wheel operates through levers on to brake blocks which are installed on the first and second drivers.

COMPLETELY streamlined, the "Cock o' the North" was built to the designs of Mr. H. N. Gresley, C.B.E., Chief Mechanical Engineer of the London and North Eastern Railway works at Doncaster, and it hauls the East Coast day expresses over the heavily graded lines between Edinburgh and Aberdeen. A giant of the iron way, its length over the buffers is 73 feet 8½ inches and its total weight in working order is 165 tons 11 cwts. Of this total, the engine weighs 110 tons 5 cwts., the tender being of 55 tons 6 cwts.

The giant driving wheels are eight in number and measure 6 feet 2 inches in diameter. The boiler, the pressure of which is 220 lbs. per square inch, has a barrel that is standard with that used on the L.N.E. "Pacific" type.

On the top of the barrel is a steam collector, which is integral with the dome and is formed of a steel casting riveted on the outside. An extra large set of steam pipes have been provided in order to ensure that the boiler pressure can be maintained in the steam chest.

In order to reduce back pressure as much as possible a double blast pipe arrangement is used. This is of a similar type to that installed on some of the largest French engines.

Railway travel a hundred years ago brought plenty of fresh air, but sought little comfort. However, in those days it was doubtful whether a great-grandfather daily donned his best stovepipe hat before roaring along at quite eight miles an hour.

(left) The interior of the driving cab of the Cock o' the North. The driver is seen at the controls while the fireman tends the glowing furnace. Special windows at the sides lend additional protection to the crew.

(Right) A narrow passage built inside the tender connects the driver's cab with the coaches at the back. Thus, relief crews are enabled to take over duty while the train is running and no interruption is caused in the work.

First published 2016

ISBN 978 0 7110 3849 3

© Andrew Hardy 2016

Published by Ian Allan Publishing

an imprint of Ian Allan Publishing Ltd, Adlestone, Surrey, KT5 2SF

Printed in Bulgaria

Visit the Ian Allan Publishing website at www.ianallanpublishing.com

Picture Credits
Every effort has been made to identify and correctly attribute photographic credits. Should any error have occurred this is entirely unintentional.

FRONT COVER *Cock o' the North* waits to back onto its train at Peterborough during running in trials in June 1934. *Transport Treasury*

BACK COVER A freshly painted No 2001 receives attention from the driver outside the paintshop at Doncaster works in May 1934. *P2SLC Collection*

HALF TITLE PAGE *Cock o' the North* is admired at Kings Cross ready for a run North. *Rail Archive Stephenson*

TITLE PAGE No 2001 is prepared for its next turn of duty. *Author's collection*

OPPOSITE A contemporary coloured cut-away illustration of No 2001. *P2SLC Collection*

CONTENTS

Acknowledgements	6
Foreword	6
About the Author	6
The A1 Steam Locomotive Trust	7
The P2 Steam Locomotive Company	7
Introduction	8
Chapter 1. The Mineral Mikado	12
Chapter 2. Gresley's Express Mikado	22
Chapter 3. Testing Times	42
Chapter 4. Mikado Evolution	54
Chapter 5. The LNER Ambassador	62
Chapter 6. The Streamlined Mikado	70
Chapter 7. Thompson Takes Over	86
Chapter 8. The Modern Mikado	96
Appendix 1	106
Appendix 2	110
Appendix 3	113
Appendix 4	114
Appendix 5	124
Bibliography	125
Index	127

ACKNOWLEDGEMENTS

Firstly I would like to thank my fiancée Gemma for her patience, help and support over the last few years whilst I have researched and written this book. Without her efforts this book would never have been completed.

I would also like to thank all my friends and colleagues at the A1 Steam Locomotive Trust, particularly Graeme Bunker, for the encouragement and opportunity to produce this work.

Likewise I would like to thank the staff at the National Railway Museum and the Science & Society Picture Library for their help and permission to use imagery from their collections along with the other photographic contributors and sources.

This book includes exclusively recoloured black and white photos by Joshua Barrett, unique artwork by Matthew Cousins and digitally restored photographs by Steve Armitage, to all of whom I would like to extend my thanks, along with all the contributors of photographic and historic material.

Lastly, but by no means least, I would like to thank my proof readers and technical experts Ian MacCabe, Roy Mears, Simon Martin, Mandy and Mark Grant and Carole Hardy.

Thank you everyone.

FOREWORD

During the production of this book I have tried to bring to the fore new and unpublished information, photographs and historical items. Many 'P2' photographs have been published before and some I have included again to help illustrate the history of the locomotives. Several of these images, however, have been brought to life using modern technology and digital colouring. These photos have been colourised by an artist using research carried out by myself and others to try to portray what would have been seen had colour photography been more advanced and widespread in the 1930s. It is not possible to make these images 100% accurate and as such they are more like an artist's interpretation of the landscape in a painting. I do hope, however, that readers will find them interesting and that they add to their enjoyment of the book.

The photographs in this publication have come from a variety of sources including private individuals, museum collections and specialist study groups. Some images of an unknown origin have been donated to the Trust over the last few years and some of these have been reproduced in this book. Every effort has been made to identify the originators and seek permission. Likewise, the content of this book has been thoroughly researched over several years but with a publication of this size it is possible that some errors or omissions may have been made.

Should readers have any information on the above points the author would be only too pleased to hear from them and can be contacted via the A1 Steam Locomotive Trust.

ABOUT THE AUTHOR

The author has held a lifelong interest with the power of steam and in particular the railway locomotive. Born in 1987 he has only ever known steam in its preservation setting and in his younger years was taken to visit many of the country's preserved heritage lines. As a teenager he participated in activates at Maidstone Model Engineering Society where his first encounter with a 'P2', albeit in 5in gauge, occurred. Andy also volunteered on the commercial side of a local heritage railway before leaving to study music at university in Leeds. Here he joined another preserved railway in the operating department, training firstly as a fireman and then progressing to driver. He eventually held a senior position and joined the railway's Council in 2008. A change of career saw him join the National Railway Museum, firstly working in education and then followed by object conservation and archiving. Whilst at the NRM the Author also worked on the museum's collection of working exhibits driving *Rocket*, *City of Truro* and other steam locomotives. A recent move has seen the author return home to Kent to further his professional career, taking up a position in the Operating Department of the Kent & East Sussex Steam Railway.

LEFT The author leaning from the cab of 'A1' *Tornado.* Mandy Grant

In 2009 he became involved with the A1 Steam Locomotive Trust as a member of the support crew for *Tornado* on both the main line and on heritage railways. It was whilst working on *Tornado* in 2013 that the author met his fiancée. In 2013 the author offered his services to help with the 'P2' locomotive project. He was appointed as an adviser to the board specialising in education and research and has undertaken much of the research work, acquiring technical and historical material to aid in the construction of the new locomotive, most notably around the valve gear.

THE A1 STEAM LOCOMOTIVE TRUST

60163 TORNADO
New Steam for the Main Line

Our mission: 'To build and operate a Peppercorn Class A1 Pacific steam locomotive for main line and preserved railway use.'

The last of the renowned Peppercorn 'A1' steam locomotives was scrapped in 1966, but now a brand new 'A1', No. 60163 *Tornado*, has been brought to life.

The A1 Steam Locomotive Trust (A1SLT) – a registered charity – has built a completely new 'A1' to the original design but with the help of the latest technology. Fitted with additional water capacity and the latest railway safety electronics, *Tornado* is fully equipped for today's main line railway.

We have thousands of supporters and the backing of the best of British business – including William Cook Cast Products, Rolls-Royce, Corus and BAe Systems – helping to raise the £3 million needed to complete *Tornado* ready for its first moves in 2008. Since then the locomotive has hauled railtours across the length and breadth of the UK and visited numerous preserved railways.

THE P2 STEAM LOCOMOTIVE COMPANY

2007 PRINCE OF WALES
Building Britain's Most Powerful Steam Locomotive

The P2 Steam Locomotive Company (P2SLC) has been established to build a new Gresley Class P2 Mikado, No 2007 *Prince of Wales*, at its Darlington Locomotive Works. Fitted with additional water capacity and the latest railway safety electronics, No 2007 will be fully equipped for tomorrow's main line railway. The Gresley Class P2 2-8-2s were the most powerful express passenger locomotives to operate in the UK. They were designed by Sir Nigel Gresley for the London & North Eastern Railway to haul 600-ton trains on the arduous Edinburgh to Aberdeen route. Six

Class P2s were built in 1934-36 but sadly the design was never fully developed and they were rebuilt by his successor Edward Thompson into ungainly 4-6-2s in 1943/4 and scrapped by 1961.

The P2SLC is a subsidiary of The A1 Steam Locomotive Trust (a registered charity), the builders and operators of world-famous new steam locomotive No 60163 *Tornado* – the first new main line steam locomotive to be built in Britain since 1960 and the first to be paid for by public subscription. The new Gresley Class P2 will, like *Tornado*, be numbered as the next in the series – No 2007. It is estimated that the new Class P2 will cost around £5 million to build over a 7-10 year period. As with *Tornado*, funds will be raised through regular monthly donations, donations dedicated to specific components, commercial sponsorship, loans and a bond issue.

To find out more please visit www.a1steam.com and www.p2steam.com

INTRODUCTION

The Main line to Aberdeen

The railways arrived in Aberdeen in 1850 with the construction of the northernmost part of what is now known as the East Coast Main Line. Services began in 1885, taking 17.5 hours from London and involving both rail and ferry journeys. With the opening of the Forth Bridge in 1890 the time was reduced to nearly 13 hours for the 523.2 miles. Until the Grouping of the principal railway companies in 1923, the East Coast route was operated by three companies, the North British Railway, North Eastern Railway and Great Northern Railway, using a pool of rolling stock bought between them. After 1923 the route came under the ownership and operation of the London & North Eastern Railway (LNER) except for the final stretch

TOP LEFT North British Atlantic *Thane of Fife* pilots a Holmes 4-4-0 on a typical heavy express leaving Aberdeen for Edinburgh during the early 1930s.
Ian Allan Library

BOTTOM LEFT No 9902 *Highland Chief* and a Reid 'D30' class 4-4-0 No 9422 *Kenilworth* pass two ex-Caledonian Railway 4-4-0s heading away from Aberdeen to Edinburgh.
Ian Allan Library

RIGHT Gradient profile of the Edinburgh to Aberdeen route.

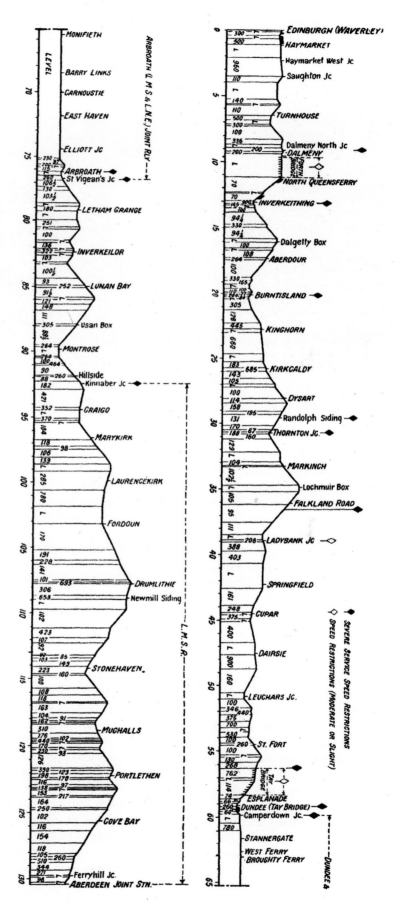

from Montrose to Edinburgh which was owned by the London, Midland & Scottish Railway (LMS) on which the LNER had running rights. In 1927, the overnight train from King's Cross to Aberdeen, leaving London at 7.30pm and arriving at Aberdeen at 7.30am, was given the title the 'Aberdonian'. This service continued throughout World War 2 as one of only four services to retain its title and continued until 1982, being one of the heaviest regular express services on the main line railway. Today it is still possible to get an overnight sleeper train from London to Aberdeen.

During the late 1920s trains over the route were being strengthened with extra vehicles, increasing the weight and putting a strain on the motive power department. In 1928 third class sleeper carriages were added to the 'Aberdonian', which necessitated regular double-heading of locomotives on the train with two sets of crews and led the Scottish Area traffic committee to consider a more powerful locomotive to be built for working the service.

Until this point, the North British 'C10' and later 'C11' class 4-4-2 Atlantics, originally designed by William Reid, had been used in traffic from 1906 and could often be seen hauling express trains to Aberdeen. At first these locomotives had given a disappointing performance until they were rebuilt with superheaters, which

transformed their operation and performance. After the Grouping the locomotives gave sterling service for the LNER until the arrival of the 'A1' class 4-6-2 Pacifics and later the 'A3' class Pacifics. The latter locomotives were permitted to work trains of 480 tons northwards and 420 tons southwards over the severe gradients of the Aberdeen route. The 'A1s', however, were not used on the Aberdeen trains, mostly being used on the Glasgow services. Unlike the Atlantics and other smaller locomotive classes, the 'A3s' were not permitted to double-head with any other locomotive over the route. The primary reason for this restriction was the weight limit applied to the Tay Bridge, a restriction that still applies to this day.

The locomotive traffic committee met in 1932 and approved a new build which would become Class P2 to help ease the double-heading problem along with five 'A3s' for unspecified operations (these would eventually be dropped). The new locomotive was included in the 1932 locomotive building program of the LNER and design started under the LNER's Chief Mechanical Engineer (CME) Herbert Nigel Gresley (later Sir Nigel Gresley).

Gresley was born on 19 June 1876 in Edinburgh but grew up in Netherseal, Derbyshire. He was the son of the local Rector, the Reverend Nigel Gresley.

ABOVE Sir Nigel Gresley, complete with pocket watch, timing one of his streamlined trains in the mid-1930s.

P2SLC Collection

After attending prep school at Barham House, St Leonards, Gresley attended Marlbrough College where he stayed until age 17, deciding to take up practical training rather than continued academic work. He became apprenticed to F. W. Webb at the London & North Western Railway's Crewe workshops during the era of the 'Races to the North'. On completion of his apprenticeship, Gresley decided his practical knowledge was lacking and arranged to spend a year in the fitting and erecting shops. Still wishing for yet more experience he moved to the Lancashire & Yorkshire Railway, where he worked in the drawing office on design work as well as running the materials test room. A move to Blackpool saw him become the Foreman of Blackpool Running Shed before a final move within the Lancashire & Yorkshire Railway under Chief Mechanical Engineer John Aspinall in the Carriage & Wagon department in 1904. A year later Gresley took up the post of Superintendent of the Great Northern Railway Carriage & Wagon department at the age of 29, starting his long association with Doncaster Works. During this time Gresley worked on carriage bogie design, articulation, steam railmotors and the design of new Royal carriages. In 1911 Gresley gained promotion and was made the Chief Mechanical Engineer of the Great Northern Railway where he soon started to show innovation in his designs including the large-boilered three-cylinder 'K3' class and later in 1922 the first three-cylinder Pacific, *Great Northern*. Gresley began the Great Northern Railway's 'Big Engine' policy of providing large engines working within their capacity. This ethos stood Gresley in good stead when he was asked to build a new, powerful locomotive for the heavy Scottish traffic.

CHAPTER 1
THE MINERAL MIKADO

In 1921 Gresley had introduced the 2-8-0 'O2' class heavy freight locomotives which were the first class of locomotive engines to use his conjugated valve gear and were designed to haul 600 ton coal trains. These three-cylinder locomotives were a development of the two-cylindered 'O1' class. Although the class eventually grew in number to 67 engines and were known for being well designed and constructed locomotives, Gresley soon found himself thinking about a more powerful heavy freight locomotive. At first, thoughts turned to a 2-10-2 design with 4ft 8in diameter coupled wheels and a wheelbase of 35ft 9in, the same size as Gresley's 'A1' Pacific's. However, some within the Civil Engineering departments showed concern about the proposal, worrying that the wheelbase would be too rigid. Alternatively, a 2-8-2 Mikado design was suggested in 1923 that allowed the locomotive to have slightly larger 5ft 2in wheels. It was this proposal that was taken forward to the Locomotive Committee in August 1923. It was stated that the cost of providing two 2-8-2 locomotives would cost £16,000, with each engine being capable of hauling 25% more wagons per train than the 2-8-0 locomotives

then used on services between Peterborough and London and between Wath Yard and Immingham. Some, however, must have thought that train loads of 100 wagons, creating a train weight of nearly 1,600 tons, were unlikely to be needed over these routes, resulting in Gresley assuring the Locomotive Committee that 'full loads can be found for them' in his submission.

On 18 August 1924 the board gave authority to Doncaster to start construction of 'Two 3-cylinder 2-8-2 Mikado 5ft 2in Coal Engines with Booster'. Design work had actually started earlier when, in April 1923, the Chief Civil Engineer gave authority for the locomotives to work on all lines between London and Shaftholme, just north of Doncaster, which had already been passed for Gresley's Pacifics. Gresley soon issued the instruction to the Doncaster draughtsman on 29 May to 'lose no time getting on with the drawings'. The following month Gresley started negotiations with The Superheater Company in New York and its UK supplier of J. Stone & Co about the possibility of fitting a booster engine below the cab to assist in starting heavy trains and their operation up steep inclines when extra power would be an

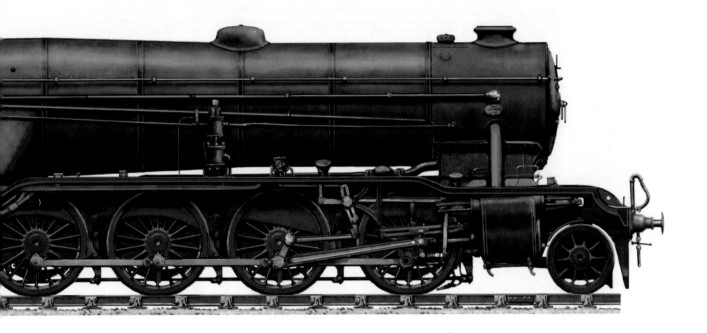

advantage. The booster engine comprised of a small auxiliary steam engine which was fitted to the trailing axles or tender of a locomotive, with the driver able to control the supplementary engine when required. This system had been pioneered in America by Harold Ingersoll of the New York Central Railroad in 1919. The new locomotives, which by now were known as the 'P1' class and allocated the numbers 2393 and 2394, were not the first LNER locomotives to be fitted with a booster. Just before the Grouping, the Great Northern Railway had acquired a standard Type C-1 booster with 10in by 12in cylinders for one of Henry Ivatt's Class C1 Atlantics, No 1419. A similar booster to this was chosen by The Superheater Company for inclusion on the 'P1' design although at first it featured a radial truck. Gresley, however, was adamant that a Cartazzi arrangement, similar to his Pacifics, would be better suited and in May 1924 the Americans agreed, admitting that it would be 'undoubtedly about the lightest form of suspension that could be worked out for the booster application to these Mikado engines'. The design of booster was expected to increase the new locomotives' tractive effort by 25%.

Frames for the locomotive were cut from 1⅛in thick steel with the rear of the locomotive receiving a double-frame section that provided a sturdy base for the locomotive's wide firebox. Frame strengthening plates were bolted and welded in place at this joint to provide extra strength. Cast frame stretchers, motion plates and the inside cylinder casting were all fitted to the frames to create a secure frame structure which, unlike some of the contemporary Pacifics of the time, never suffered from any problems often associated with locomotive frames. The cylinders were cast as three separate castings with the outside cylinders angled at 1 in 40 whilst the inside cylinder was inclined at 1 in 8 to clear the axle of the leading coupled wheels. Gresley's conjugated valve gear was once again used on the locomotives based on the arrangement initially used on his 'O2' class 2-8-0 mineral locomotives and developed on his 'A1' class Pacifics.

The locomotive was equipped with Gresley's patent swing link suspension on the front pony truck, which although it caused problems on some of Gresley's other locomotives seems to have worked satisfactorily on the two 'P1' engines. The coupled driving wheels featured

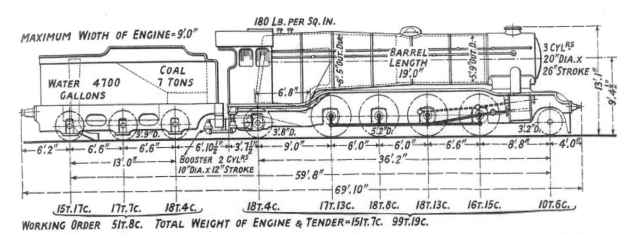

MAXIMUM WIDTH OF ENGINE=9'0"

180 LB. PER SQ. IN.

BARREL
LENGTH
19'0"

3 CYL.RS
20"DIA.X
26"STROKE

WATER 4700
GALLONS

COAL
7 TONS

6'.5"OUT. DIA.

5'.9"OUT. D.

13'.1"

9'.4½"

6'.8"

3'.9"D.   3'.8"D.   5'.2"D.   3'.2"D.

6'.2" — 6'.6" — 6'.6" — 6'.10½" — 3'.7½" — 9'.0" — 6'.0" — 6'.0" — 6'.6" — 8'.8" — 4'.0"

13'.0"   BOOSTER 2 CYL.RS   36'.2"
              10"DIA.x 12"STROKE

59'.8"

69'.10"

15T.17C.   17T.7C.   18T.4C.   18T.4C.   17T.13C.   18T.8C.   18T.13C.   16T.15C.   10T.6C.

WORKING ORDER 51T.8C. TOTAL WEIGHT OF ENGINE & TENDER=151T.7C. 99T.19C.

HEATING SURFACE, TUBES—							SUPERHEATER ELEMENTS	...	...	...	32–1½ IN. DIA. OUTS.
LARGE AND SMALL	...	...	...	...	2,715·0 SQ. FT.		LARGE TUBES ...	... 32–5½ IN. DIA. OUTS.			19 FT.
FIREBOX ...	...	...	...	...	215·0 "		SMALL TUBES ...	... 168–2¼ IN. DIA. OUTS.		BET. TUBEPLATES	
TOTAL (EVAPORATIVE)	...	...	...	...	2,930·0 "		GRATE AREA ...	...	...	...	41·25 SQ. FT.
SUPERHEATER ...	...	...	...	...	525·0 "		TRACTIVE EFFORT (AT 85 PER CENT. B.P.)			...	38,500 LB.*
COMBINED HEATING SURFACES	...	...	...	3,455·0 "						

* With booster in action tractive effort is increased to 47,000 lb.

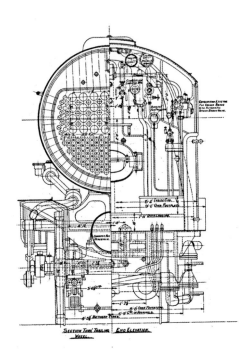

SECTION THRO' TRAILING END ELEVATION.
      WHEEL.

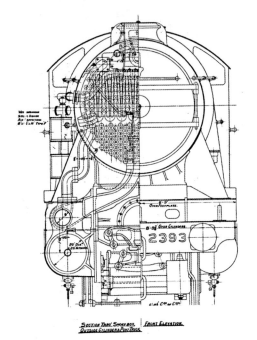

2393

SECTION THRO' SMOKE BOX. FRONT ELEVATION.
OUTSIDE CYLINDER & PONY TRUCK.

ABOVE Diagram for 'P1' class showing general statistics and sizes. *NRM/SSPL*

LEFT General arrangement drawings of 'P1' class 2-8-2 locomotive (see also front endpapers). *NRM/SSPL*

laminated spring suspension and were fitted with equalising beams between the springs to help ensure a more even weight distribution. However, these were removed from the two locomotives during April and May 1940. Lubrication to the axleboxes was supplied by a mechanical lubricator mounted on the driver's side running plate. The trailing wheels featured the Cartazzi arrangement with laminated springs fitted with the booster mentioned earlier.

In an unusual move the engine was fitted with steam reversing equipment between the frames to aid the driver in adjusting the cut-off setting and reversing the locomotive. The locomotive was also fitted with steam brakes operating on the engine and tender and equipped with a vacuum ejector for working vacuum-braked freight stock.

The new locomotives featured the same 180psi boiler as the 'A1' Pacifics operating at the time to ensure maximum interchangeability. Each locomotive, however, was slightly different. The Superheater Company that supplied the booster engine design recommended that the

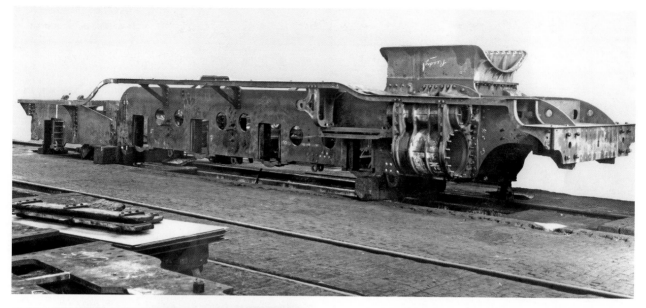

TOP The erected frames for the first 'P1' engine. *NRM/SSPL*

ABOVE The trailing truck booster engine fitted under the cab floor. The steam supply pipe with its three troublesome articulated couplings can clearly be seen. *NRM/SSPL*

steaming ability of the Gresley boiler could be further improved by the addition of one of their 'E double'-type superheaters which would heat the steam to 700 degrees Fahrenheit as opposed to the 575 degrees Fahrenheit thought to be produced by the standard 'A1' boiler. Two sets of superheaters were ordered, one set being installed on No 2394 whilst the other set was fitted to 'A1' No 2562 *Isinglass*. This fitting required two anti-vacuum or 'snifting' valves to be fitted behind the chimney on the top of the boiler. No 2933 was fitted with the standard-pattern Robinson 32-element superheater and single snifting valve. Tests were carried out with 'A1' No 2562 to examine the improvements produced by the E-type superheater. The temperatures recorded, however, were only 31 degrees higher than on the

locomotive fitted with a Robinson-type superheater. With costs of fitting the superheater and maintenance taken into account it was decided to stay with the Robinson-type superheater as standard and in November 1931 No 2934 was fitted with the standard equipment. The boilers were fitted with Davies & Metcalfe No 10 exhaust steam injectors on the fireman's side and No 10 (No 11 in the case of 2394 with the E-type superheater) live steam injectors on the driver's side. No 2394 was fitted with an experimental soot blower but this was removed in 1936 after the Locomotive Running Superintendents decided to do away with them on all locomotives. In November 1942 No 2394 received a new 'A3'-type boiler working at an increased pressure of 220psi with No 2393 following suit in January 1943.

The cab design was identical to the 'A1' Pacifics of the time. From the outset the locomotives were right-hand drive with the steam reverser, booster engine gear, vacuum and steam brakes fitted within easy reach of the driver's seated position. The standard arrangement of LNER pull-out-type regulator was fitted on both sides of the cab. At first only wooden seat bases were fitted but these were modified in early 1937 to include seat backs, at which time the cut-out in the cab side was reduced to help prevent draughting.

In operation, the booster engine had to be operated before the locomotive reached 10mph and disengaged before it reached 21mph. To control the booster a Westinghouse air compressor of 8in by 8½in stroke was fitted on the locomotive's right-hand running plate. This

controlled the equipment that allowed the gears on the booster engine to be meshed in and out of sync with the trailing wheels and could only be operated when the engine was in full forward gear, automatically cutting out when the engine was notched up.

Tenders for the locomotives were ordered on 12 February 1925, as order No 46, and allocated the numbers 5293 and 5294. These tenders held 4,700 gallons and were based around the eight-wheeled Pacific design including the same tank arrangement and storage for fire irons. Other features from the Darlington-designed 4,200-gallon Group Standard tender were also used including the double-framed chassis. The tender sides did not feature coal rails; instead a solid coping plate was fitted at the top. The coal space was self-trimming to aid the fireman whilst the water tank also incorporated a well between the frames to ensure maximum capacity. Water pick-up equipment was fitted to the tender to allow the locomotive to take water on the move. The front of the tender below footplate level, however, contained differences to any other tender, incorporating a large overhang to allow space for the steam pipes and other fittings required at the rear of the booster engine fitted on the rear of the engine portion of the locomotive. When completed the locomotives were finished in the standard goods engine livery of plain black with red lining with 'LNER' on the tender, later being changed to just 'NE' during the war.

No 2393 was completed in June 1925, just in time for the Stockton & Darlington Centenary celebrations in early July, appearing alongside all the other celebrity locomotives including *Locomotion*, *Aerolite*, the new LNER Gresley 'A1' No 2563 *William Whitelaw*, the new LNER Garratt, a GWR 'Castle' and even a Stroudley 'Terrier'. No 2394 was completed in November that year with the total cost of both engines being £20,986, nearly £5,000 more than estimated.

The engines were soon put to work hauling coal trains between New England yard in Peterborough and Ferme Park near Hornsey. From the outset the locomotives worked well but there were reports of axleboxes running hot when the engines were worked hard. This resulted in footplate crews working the engine with a partially open regulator and around 50% cut-off as a regular occurrence. On 6 September 1925 No 2393 was put onto a special 1,575-ton test train. This was the first time a 'P1' locomotive had been allowed to work the type of train it had been designed for, the train being formed of the LNER dynamometer car, 101 wagons and a 20-ton brake van. On leaving New England the booster engine was not used as there was concern that the starting force of the engine may have been too powerful for the dynamometer car spring. On starting the maximum effort required was 12 tons, well within the 18-ton limit of the spring. After a short stop at Offord the locomotive was restarted, this time with the booster engine in operation although it took some distance to get the booster engine to fully engage. Full use of the booster engine was not made because of the driver's reluctance to fully open the regulator; however, after Biggleswade and after the booster was disengaged the locomotive was run at 45% cut-off (still less than the test engineer's desired 30%) and full

regulator. On arrival at Cambridge Junction the leading right-hand axlebox was found to be hot and required attention. Once again the locomotive was restarted; this time a pull of 14 tons was recorded by the dynamometer car. The locomotive continued its journey to Ferme Park in a gentle and uneventful manner where the axlebox was found to still be running hot. The tests showed that the locomotive had a very high coal consumption of around 150lb per mile and that the booster engine could only be used to full advantage on the heaviest trains of around 1,600 tons. It was also decided that the issue of how the locomotives were driven must be addressed as the style of driving that persisted because of the hot axlebox issue resulted in the boosters again not being used in an efficient manner. Retraining was called for, with crews being instructed to operate the locomotive at around 35% cut-off and a wider-opened regulator. This instruction, however, was not always followed mainly due to the fear of causing hotboxes.

The fact that the locomotives gave their best work on 1,600-ton trains gave rise to a problem for the Operating Department. The engines worked their own special diagrams and instructions were issued in the working timetables accordingly (see Appendices). Trains of 100 wagons had to be very carefully planned and handled. Many of the loops and refuge sidings on

the railway could not handle such long trains so the trips had to be carefully planned to run on the goods or slow lines to allow other workings to pass. Most of the ECML at this time featured a number of bottlenecks which would take another few decades to improve to four lines and alleviate the problem. If the train had to be detained for any reason it would have to be held on a running line, thus causing delay to any services behind it. This became particularly difficult when extra services, like holiday excursions, were operated. Likewise, in the winter months, when the demand for coal in London was higher and extra trains were operating, the yards at Ferme Park could not turn around the required trains quickly enough, causing delays in the loading and unloading of waiting trains. This was eased somewhat a few years later when a reception road capable of holding three 80-wagon trains was built nearby. With the railway continuing to develop faster timetabled services and the introduction of colour light signalling, allowing for shorter block sections, the available paths for 100-wagon trains greatly diminished or disappeared. This resulted in the locomotives hauling trains far below their ideal loading of 1,600 tons resulting in the engines running uneconomically and thus becoming a victim of their own success in the haulage stakes.

The engines were seemingly held in high esteem by the Operating Department and

ABOVE Standing next to the coal stage at New England shed the equipment for the booster engine can be seen in this image of No 2934. *Ian MacCabe Collection*

TOP RIGHT No 2393 on exhibition at Hitchin in 1937. *Ian Allan Library*

RIGHT No 2394 with booster in operation hauling a heavy coal train to Ferme Park. *IanAllan Library*

footplate crews and in October 1926 the Locomotive Running Superintendents recommended that four elderly 0-8-0 'Long Tom' locomotives should be withdrawn and replaced by a further four 'P1' locomotives. Unfortunately the recommendation was not carried forward and no further 'P1s' were built.

The engines were occasionally displayed at LNER open days. During May 1936 No 2394 was exhibited at Cambridge whilst No 2393 appeared not only at the Stockton & Darlington Centenary exhibition mentioned earlier but also at a public exhibition at New Barnet on 5 and 6 June 1937.

Unfortunately, the booster engine often gave trouble with a regular fault that saw the articulated cast-iron steam pipes (that were designed to allow for vertical and horizontal movement) breaking at the ball and socket joint. This required a new casting, which had to be sent from Doncaster to the locomotive's location and often meant the engines were out of service for a few days whilst requiring

ABOVE Engine No 2394
awaiting scrapping at
Doncaster Works.
Ian Allan Library

RIGHT With the fireman
hard at work No 2393
works a heavy southbound
train near Hatfield.
Ian Allan Library

attention. It is thought that the failure was caused by the over-tightening of the joints. Whilst running on normal lines this was probably not a problem but at New England depot the engines were often turned on a sharp turning triangle which, even with the engine negotiating slowly, caused undue stresses and strains on the joints. The problem was never properly resolved and in April 1937 No 2394 lost its booster equipment. No 2393 continued with a booster for another year, being fitted in February 1937 with the booster equipment from 'C1' class No 4419 before it was eventually removed completely in May 1938. In the years running up to the removal of the booster equipment the locomotives had been running

with reduced loads and the boosters had generally not been used. The loss of the equipment does not seem to have been a disappointment for the footplate crews but may have been for the New England shed fitters who often received overtime pay whilst working on repairing the joints.

The 'P1' locomotives were never designed or envisaged to work passenger trains. However, during the early design stages of the express passenger 'P2' 2-8-2 engine, No 2394 was trialled on the 7.45am King's Cross to Doncaster stopping train to assess the suitability of a 2-8-2 wheel arrangement for passenger work. The train ran as far as Peterborough with the 'P1' and attained speeds of 65mph although the fireman was

reported to have remarked that he was glad the engine was not working through to Doncaster on account of the work required firing when running at speed. Occasionally during the war years the engines found themselves working local pick-up goods trains on the Great Northern main lines although it was reported that drivers unused to the extra power offered by a 'P1' could occasionally break couplings whilst shunting with the engines.

Both 'P1' engines were withdrawn in July 1945 by Edward Thompson who had succeeded Gresley as CME. Thompson wanted to standardise locomotive designs and saw no place for a class of two unique engines, especially when the work they were designed to do never developed, or could not be handled without causing disruption to the wider railway network. However, the engines were not completely scrapped. The boiler of each engine was reused to help rebuild two locomotives – Nos 2557 and 2565 – from 'A1' to 'A3' class. After overhaul and with suitable modifications carried out, the tenders were once again put to use with two Class B2 locomotives. Unusually, the frames of No 2393 were not scrapped, instead being used as a boiler carrier at Doncaster Works. This saw the sad end of Gresley's mineral Mikados after a relatively short life of only two decades. Incidentally, Oliver Bulleid is on record as saying that of all the designs of Sir Nigel Gresley the 'P1' class was the most attractive and his favourite Gresley design.

CHAPTER 2

GRESLEY'S EXPRESS MIKADO

Although a variety of other locomotives had been tried on the Edinburgh to Aberdeen route it quickly became evident to Gresley that a new locomotive would be required to meet the demands of the Scottish Area Operating Department and the traffic it was expected to work.

Gresley sought permission to design a new engine specifically for this traffic and with permission given by the LNER Locomotive and Traffic Committee he set about designing the new locomotive. The first diagram was issued on 30 March 1932 showing a 2-8-2 version of his 'A3' class fitted with 6ft 2in driving wheels. Other drawings were issued over the coming months with various features being added or removed. Gresley also consulted his Special Assistant O. V. S. Bulleid about the project.

Oliver Vaughan Snell Bulleid was born in Invercargill, New Zealand, on 19 September 1882, his parents having emigrated there in 1875. Shortly before his seventh birthday Bulleid's father died of pleurisy, which resulted in Bulleid and his younger siblings and mother returning to Wales, his mother's native home. Bulleid grew

up in Llanfyllin near Oswestry before attending Spa College in Bridge of Allan, Stirlingshire. This was followed by Accrington Technical College where he developed the practical skills first learnt in the workshop of his Uncle William.

His mother had made arrangements for him to return to New Zealand to study for the legal profession. However, his cousin, the Reverend Edgar Lee, did not want to see him leave and arranged for him to attend a meeting with the Great Northern Railway's (GNR) Locomotive Superintendant Henry Ivatt, who was one of his parishioners. Following his interview he was offered an apprenticeship starting on 21 January 1901. After successfully completing his four-year apprenticeship which was spent learning as many practical skills as possible, along with a short spell as assistant to the railway's Locomotive Running Superintendent, Bulleid was promoted to be personal assistant to Mr Wintour, the Doncaster Works Manager.

Bulleid left the GNR in 1908 to take a job with the Westinghouse Electric Corporation in Paris, the same year that he married Marjorie Ivatt, the

daughter of H. A. Ivatt. They lived in Paris for several years and Bulleid took the time to become fluent in the local language before moving to Turin when he was appointed engineer for the 1911 trade exhibition.

In 1912 he rejoined the GNR, becoming Gresley's Personal Assistant, who had just been appointed the new Chief Mechanical Engineer. From 1914 to 1919 he volunteered for war service working on military railway projects on the Continent. He once again returned to Doncaster, this time as the Manager of the Carriage & Wagon works, before becoming Assistant Carriage & Wagon Superintendent in 1920. With the Grouping in 1923, Gresley became CME of the LNER and asked Bulleid to become his Special Assistant working on a variety of projects including carriage underframe and wagon welding.

The early designs for Gresley's new locomotive class for the Edinburgh to Aberdeen line were submitted to the various engineers and departments across the LNER for approval along with those of the London Midland & Scottish Railway who owned the last section of the line from Kinnaber

Junction (made famous during the Races to the North) to Aberdeen. On 25 May 1932 the design was agreed in principle and approved for development. Design work continued right through until February 1933 when Engine Order No 330 was issued to Doncaster works to construct two 'P2' class engines. This was amended on 13 April 1933 to just one locomotive.

Experience had already been gained from the construction of the 'P1' class locomotives and Gresley had also been taking a keen interest in the 2-8-2 Mikado arrangement on both the European Continent and in North America. Gresley was particularly impressed with the engines working over the Rocky Mountains in Canada, which he witnessed and experienced whilst travelling there in 1929 with his daughter Violet, shortly after the passing of his wife Ethel from cancer. Gresley was devastated by his wife's death and the trip to Canada came about after advice that he should take a long holiday from work. On his return from Canada Gresley moved house and returned to work although he never truly recovered from Ethel's passing.

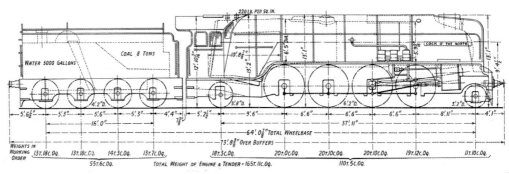

ABOVE LEFT O. V. S. Bulleid, Special Assistant to Gresley. *P2SLC Collection*

ABOVE RIGHT An initial diagram issued by the CME department prior to construction of the locomotive. *NRM/SSPL*

RIGHT Letter from R.A. Thom stating that the relevant LNER Engineers had accepted the new locomotive design and authorising detailed design work to take place. *NRM/SSPL*

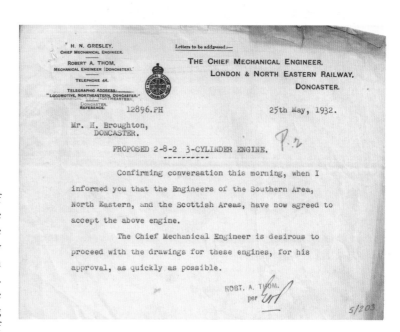

The Mikado arrangement gave four pairs of coupled driving wheels to transmit the locomotive's power and provided the best possible adhesion for working heavy trains. The front pony truck gave space for the large cylinder block which would be necessary for such a large locomotive. Some engineers may have preferred a front bogie truck but this would have necessitated increasing the locomotives length with a subsequent loss of adhesion over the coupled wheels, something Gresley was not willing to sacrifice.

The front pony truck was fitted with Gresley's swing link system to control sideways movement which equalises the weight on the leading set of coupled wheels. It is interesting to note this choice of control for the pony truck as at the time the Pacific bogies were being converted away from swing link control to helical side control springs. Bert Spencer, Gresley's Chief Technical Assistant, tried to persuade Gresley to adopt the Bissell truck arrangement after being impressed with the Southern Railway's 'River' class tank locomotives, which had been tested between St Neots and Huntingdon at speeds in the low 80s during 1927.

However, Gresley knew the swing link trucks were cheaper to construct and decided not to deviate from the norm, basing the arrangement for the 'P2' on the layout he used for the 'K3' locomotives some years previously. The rear of the locomotive sat over a trailing truck fitted

with Cartazzi axleboxes, allowing a wide firebox to be placed above it. The engine's driving wheels were 6ft 2in diameter spaced at 6ft 6in apart. The front pony wheels were 3ft 2in whilst the trailing axle was 3ft 8in.

Overall the wheelbase of the locomotive was less than 38ft (compared to 38ft 9in of the 'A3' Pacifics). The frames for the engine were cut from 1⅛in steel plate with work starting on their construction in February 1934. Each of the main frames were assembled from three pieces, the front section joining between the leading and second set of coupled wheels and the rear portion joined near to the position of the firebox. The width of the frames varied along the length of the locomotive with various reinforcing plates added to give strength to several sections. Cast steel stretchers were added between the frames along with motion plates, dragboxes and other frame elements. Finally, the axlebox hornblocks were attached to the frames, and then carefully aligned using the optical method then in use at Doncaster.

ABOVE The frames for No 2001 are cut out by hand, February 1934. *NRM/SSPL*

An enlarged version of Gresley's 'A3'-type Pacific boiler (Diagram 94HP) was chosen for the new locomotive which was designated Diagram 106. The boiler barrel consisted of two sections: a taper section of 8ft 7⅜in that tapered from 6ft 5in at the firebox end to 5ft 10¾in and a second section, 11ft 9⅝in long by 5ft 9⅝in, fitted to the inside of the narrow end of the taper section, giving a total barrel length of 19ft.

The front and rear tubeplates were fitted 18ft 11¾in apart and fitted with 121 standard tubes and 43 superheater flue tubes. Superheating was provided by 43 'sine wave' superheater elements fitted to a MLS superheater header. The sine wave elements undulate along the length of the superheater tubes and were designed to create a turbulent steam flow to stop the build up of deposits on the tube walls. These deposits would affect the efficiency of the tubes in transferring their heat into the steam.

The external length of the firebox was 10ft 9in with an inner firebox size of 7ft 2in long by 6ft 11¾in wide. This gave a total firebox grate area

BELOW The completed boiler for *Cock o' the North* posed for a works photograph. *NRM/SSPL*

ABOVE TOP Following their cutting the frame plate edges are machined at Doncaster Works. *NRM/SSPL*

ABOVE CENTRE The frames waiting for the monobloc cylinder casting to be fitted. *NRM/SSPL*

ABOVE The locomotive's main frames fitted with the monobloc cylinders and cast motion bracket assembled inside Doncaster Locomotive Works. *NRM/SSPL*

of 50sq ft which Gresley believed was the largest manageable size for a single fireman. The firebox crown was just less than 6ft 9in above the foundation ring at the front of the firebox sloping to just over 6ft at the rear of the firebox. Gresley also incorporated a perforated steam-collector inside the dome. This was fed by a series of ½in slots, 18 in number, in the top of the barrel plate. Steam collectors were afterwards fitted to all new boilers for his big engines including the 'A3', 'A4', 'P2' and 'V2' classes and colloquially became known as 'banjo domes'. As built, the total boiler heating surface was 3,490sq ft, made up of 237sq ft for the firebox, 1,354sq ft from the tubes, 1,122sq ft from the flue tubes and 695sq feet from the superheater elements.

The engine would have three large cylinders of 21in diameter and 26in stroke. However, unlike most locomotives where the cylinders would be cast individually, the cylinder block for the 'P2' was made as a single-piece monobloc casting. The monobloc casting incorporated the three cylinder bores, valve chests and steam exhaust passages into one large casting that could then be machined prior to fitting to the locomotive.

The Gorton Works foundry of the NE section of the LNER had become expert in casting monobloc cylinders and for many years had provided castings for many designs of three-cylinder locomotives including Greley's own 'V1' and 'V3' class 2-6-2 tanks and 'V2' tender engines. Monobloc castings were advantageous to locomotive engineers because of the reduced weight compared to traditional cast cylinders and also for the smaller number of bolts and

steam-tight joints required to hold the cylinders to the locomotives main frames.

As one casting it was also easier to accurately align the cylinders to each other using precise machinery in the machine shop rather than during the correction stage on the workshop floor.

The cylinders for the 'P2' locomotives were cast at Gorton Works, Manchester under the direction of R. Thom. To make the casting, wooden patterns of the outside surfaces along with core boxes for the inside surfaces were made from drawings supplied by Doncaster Works. The wooden pattern was then transferred into a sand mould ready for pouring. Both the drawings and wooden pattern were produced proportionately larger than required to account for contraction of the metal whilst cooling. For convenience during pouring and because a greater portion of

TOP LEFT & RIGHT The inner firebox is lifted into the upturned outer wrapper ready for the fitting of stays. *NRM/SSPL*

ABOVE Boiler and smokebox assembly erected inside Doncaster Works. *NRM/SSPL*

LEFT Inside and outside views of the perforated steam collector. Note the tanks on top of the boiler for the ACFI feedwater heater. *NRM/SSPL*

ABOVE Front view of the monobloc cylinder casting. *NRM/SSPL*

the metal was in the upper part of the finished casting the mould was made with the cylinder bores uppermost.

Once the metal had been poured it was then allowed to stand for three days whilst it completely cooled before being removed from the mould. Only minor fettling was required at that stage, consisting of removing any remaining sand and general trimming and cleaning. The casting was then transferred to the machine shop where cylinders and steam passageways could be bored out to the relevant sizes. The finished castings were then transferred to Doncaster for fitting on the locomotive.

Bulleid had wanted to see the new locomotive incorporate poppet valves and had persuaded

Gresley to look into their application on such a large engine. At the time the licence for the Lentz valve gear in the UK was held by Associated Locomotive Equipment Ltd and in consequence of this the company sent a draughtsman on 17 July 1933 to meet with Mr Broughton, the LNER Chief Draughtsman, and discuss the cylinder design. Gresley later instructed Broughton to 'finish the thing off' with poppet valves as soon as possible. However, it seems that the first cylinders cast for the new locomotive were for traditional piston valves and when Gresley visited Gorton Works on 24 October 1933 to view this first pair of 'P2' cylinders he made the decision to change the design and equip them with experimental Lentz poppet valves after

RIGHT Sectional drawing for the 'P2' monobloc cylinders. *P2SLC Collection*

BELOW Letter from R. A. Thom to H. Broughton describing Gresley's decision to change the engine from piston to poppet valves. *NRM/SSPL*

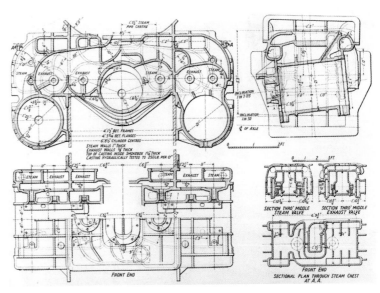

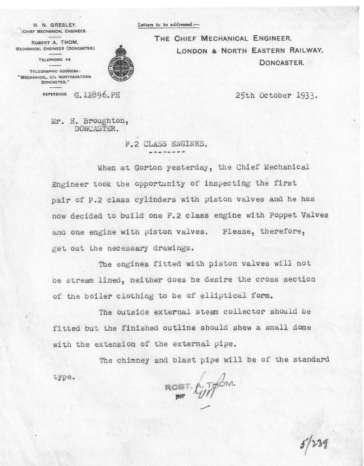

much persuading and lobbying by Oliver Bulleid. An instruction was then issued by Gresley for the drawings to be prepared and a new set of cylinders cast and eventually for these to be fitted to the new locomotive.

This engine would not, however, be the first on which the LNER had experimented with using poppet valves. The first locomotive in Britain to use poppet valves had, in fact, been a miniature railway locomotive named *River Esk* used on the Ravenglass & Eskdale Railway in Cumbria. The locomotive had been designed by Henry Greenly and was built by Davey Paxman and Co of Colchester who at the time held the patent rights for the Lentz valve gear. The locomotive was constructed in 1923 and it was also during this year, according to Bulleid, who worked closely with the CME on utilising poppet valves, that Gresley decided to investigate the possibilities of poppet valves and their uses on standard gauge locomotives. Gresley and Greenly were on friendly terms (Greenly built several locomotives for the Romney, Hythe & Dymchurch Railway which were based on Gresley's express engines) and one wonders whether discussions between the two of them had influenced Gresley's decision to try the Lentz valve gear.

The first standard gauge locomotive to be fitted with Lentz poppet valves was a 'J20' class 0-6-0 goods locomotive. This engine, No 8280, was completed at Stratford Works in March 1925 and equipped with Lentz oscillating cam valvegear supplied by Davey Paxman for the purposes of assessing the advantages of steam distribution and coal consumption produced by the Lentz valves. After two years in operation, it was reported that it had 'been in continuous service and the poppet valve gear has not given the slightest trouble nor have any repairs or renewals to any part of it been required'. The engine continued with Lentz valves until being rebuilt with conventional piston valves

in September 1937. The trial must have been considered a success as it paved the way for poppet valves to be tried on larger express locomotives.

Following the successful trials it was decided to fit Lentz oscillating cam valves to a 'B12' class 4-6-0 express locomotive. In general, the equipment used was similar to the 'J20', however

ABOVE 'D49' No 211 *The York and Ainsty* **fitted with Lentz valve gear.** *Ian Allan Library.*

this time the valve chests were made complete with the two cylinders in one casting rather than as a separate bolt-on unit. Entering service in December 1926, the locomotive was utilised on express passenger work and gave good performances. In a paper to the Institution of Locomotive Engineers Bulleid noted that the poppet valve gear had been performing consistently well but conceded that, being the first engines fitted with this gear, they were well looked after and often worked by the same drivers.

From 1928 to 1930 the LNER converted another five 'B12' locomotives to Lentz valves. Due to a shortage of locomotives in 1927 a further batch of ten 'B12s' were ordered from the Manchester firm of Beyer Peacock. These locomotives were originally planned to have piston valves however, after the order was placed, Gresley decided to fit them with the Lentz valves. This led to a dispute with the makers with both sides refusing to cover the extra cost required until eventually the LNER agreed to pay £1,500, half the sum requested by Beyer Peacock. The Lentz Equipment was again supplied by Davey Paxman and the locomotives were completed between August and October 1928.

Unfortunately, the application of poppet valves on these locomotives was not a success as it was found that the economy on water compared to their piston valve sisters was marginal. Another major problem was the tendency of the monobloc cylinder castings to crack, leading to the requirement for very expensive replacements. This was probably due to the fact that the inlet and exhaust ports were too close together and the temperature between the inlet and exhaust steam led to excessive stress in the casting.

The problem was so serious that the LNER started converting some of the 1928 batch of locomotives back to piston valves in November 1931. Over 16 of the Lentz valve locomotives had

either been converted back to the original piston valves and valve gear or rebuilt as 'B12/3s' with long-travel piston valves by January 1934. It should be noted, however, that the problems with these locomotives were perhaps more attributable to the cylinder casting cracking than to the operation of the poppet valves and valve gear itself.

During the same time as the 'B12' locomotives were being fitted with the Lentz valves, the LNER decided to fit a number of the new 'D49' 'Shire' class locomotives with Lentz valves which were being built at Darlington works. Like the 'B12' locomotives, these engines were fitted with oscillating cam-operated valves driven by slightly modified Walschaerts valve gear and received the classification 'D49/3'. The poppet valves were housed in individual valve boxes bolted to the top of each cylinder. These had four valves controlling admission and exhaust at each end of the cylinder. Like the 'B12s' the oscillating cam arrangement did not appear to be a great success and during 1938 when the locomotives required new cylinders they were rebuilt as D49/1s locomotives with conventional piston and valves.

Gresley, however, thought a new form of operating mechanism, rather than the usual Walschaerts or Stephenson's motion, was required to gain the full potential of the Lentz poppet valves. A rotational motion would be ideal as this could be operated by the turning of the locomotive's wheels through a shaft and gear box. Gresley invited Lentz Patents Ltd to design a rotary valve gear for a three-cylinder engine in collaboration with the LNER. The new design consisted of a rotating camshaft running across the length with the three cylinders which were all cast in line. The cams operated all the inlet and exhaust valves, giving any valve event desired. This new valve gear had five fixed cut-off positions. The first two 'Shire' class engines to be fitted with the Lentz rotary cam valve gear were

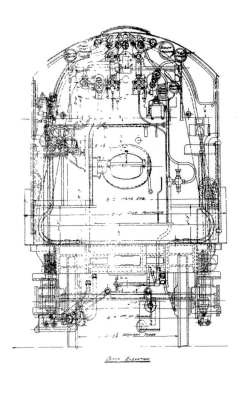

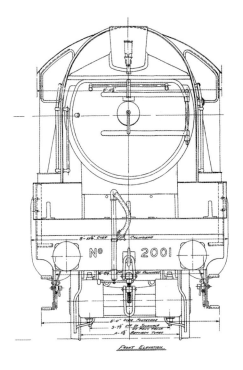

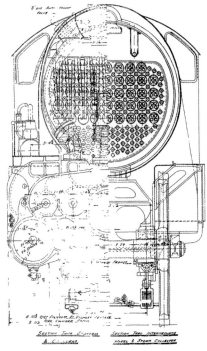

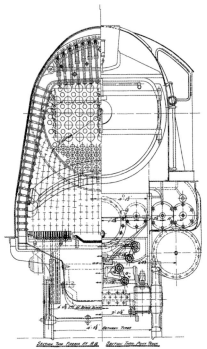

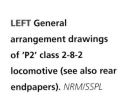

No 336 *Buckinghamshire* and No 352 *Leicestershire*, these being completed in early 1929. The running department soon indicated that they were performing much better than the locomotives fitted with oscillating cams and as such all future 'D49s' were built with the rotary cam gear, these being classified 'D49/2'. In total 42 locomotives were built and fitted with the rotary cams between 1929 and 1935. These engines were not named after shires but after fox hunts and to bring the first two engines into line they were renamed in 1932 as *The Quorn* and *The Meynell*.

The five-stepped cams soon proved to be insufficient and a trial was made at first in October 1932 with a handmade camshaft that allowed infinitely variable cut-off between 15% and 84% and later with a seven-stepped fixed

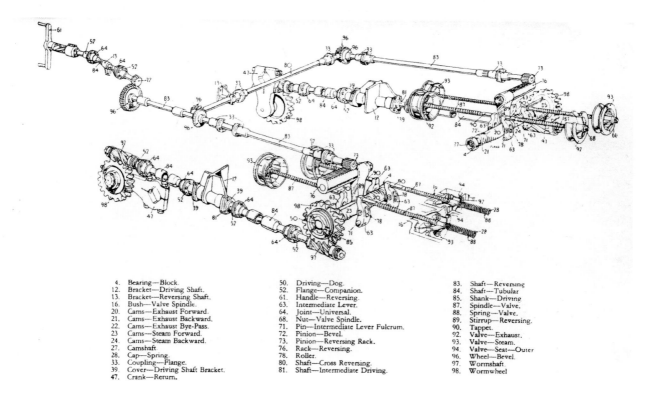

4.	Bearing—Block.	50.	Driving—Dog.	83.	Shaft—Reversing.	
12.	Bracket—Driving Shaft.	52.	Flange—Companion.	84.	Shaft—Tubular	
13.	Bracket—Reversing Shaft.	61.	Handle—Reversing.	85.	Shank—Driving	
16.	Bush—Valve Spindle.	63.	Intermediate Lever.	87.	Spindle—Valve.	
20.	Cams—Exhaust Forward.	64.	Joint—Universal.	88.	Spring—Valve.	
21.	Cams—Exhaust Backward.	68.	Nut—Valve Spindle.	89.	Stirrup—Reversing.	
22.	Cams—Exhaust Bye-Pass.	71.	Pin—Intermediate Lever Fulcrum.	90.	Tappet.	
23	Cams—Steam Forward.	72.	Pinion—Bevel.	92.	Valve—Exhaust.	
24.	Cams—Steam Backward.	73.	Pinion—Reversing Rack.	93.	Valve—Steam.	
27.	Camshaft.	76.	Rack—Reversing.	94.	Valve-Seat—Outer	
28.	Cap—Spring.	78.	Roller.	96.	Wheel—Bevel.	
33.	Coupling—Flange.	80.	Shaft—Cross Reversing.	97.	Wormshaft	
39.	Cover—Driving Shaft Bracket.	81.	Shaft—Intermediate Driving.	98.	Wormwheel	
47.	Crank—Return.					

cut-off design in (1934), with the latter eventually fitted to 27 of the locomotives. It is not known why the infinitely variable cut-off design was not used as no records of problems or failures are known of but it was soon removed from the trial locomotive in April 1934. The engines were used across the NE and Scottish areas of the LNER giving good service on express and local passenger trains, retaining their rotary cam Lentz gear until withdrawal and eventual scrapping between 1957 and 1961, a service time broadly similar to their piston valve cousins

The opportunity was also taken to fit two 'C7' Atlantic class engines with Lentz rotary cam gear in 1933 and 1934. These engines had been used by Gresley to test a number of other pieces of auxiliary equipment and were the only engines of this type to be fitted with poppet valves. The engines both ran well with a crisp exhaust beat but the overall improvement and cost savings did not warrant the conversion of any more engines of this type. The engines, which were classified C7/2, kept their Lentz valve gear until withdrawal and scrapping.

The new 'P2' engine, was the largest locomotive in Britain that would be equipped with the Lentz valve gear. The rotary cam version was used once again with an arrangement of two camshafts. One camshaft operated the left-hand cylinder and the inlet of the inside cylinder whilst the second camshaft worked the right-hand cylinder and the exhaust of the inside cylinder. The motion was derived from a skew gear which transferred the motion from the driving wheels to a shaft and thence to the camshaft situated at right angles to the locomotive across the top of the cylinder block. Mounted on the camshafts were six scroll cams, one for the inlet and exhaust of each cylinder. These scroll cams gave an infinitely variable cut-off setting between 10% and 70% in forward gear and 31% and 70% in reverse gear.

The variation in cut-off was controlled by a wheel-type reverser inside the cab mounted on the driver's side. Each cylinder was equipped with four valves, two inlets and two outlets, which featured spring-loaded valve spindles holding them closed. The spindles each had a pair of rollers which followed the cam profile as it turned, opening and closing the valve. When the engine was in mid-gear the inlet valves were kept shut whilst the exhaust valves were open to assist the engine when coasting. The greatest advantage of this system was the ability to give perfect valve events across the entire range of cut-off positions. The poppet valves operated in a manner that allowed a slow opening followed by a quicker movement to the fully open position, and a quick closing movement followed by a slower action at the point of closure, giving a nice even flow of steam with no throttling through partly open ports as you would find on

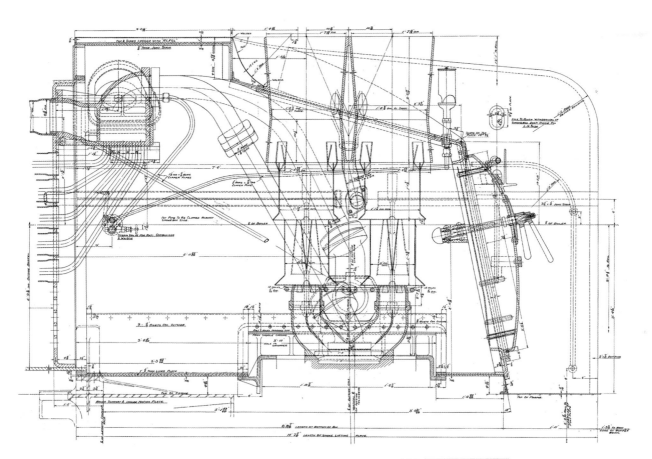

the more traditional valve gears. The gear also gave identical valve events when the engine was running in the reverse direction, something not possible from a radial gear such as Walschaerts.

To accompany the poppet valves and to ensure that the most efficient use of steam was made, Gresley sought to make the engine's steam circuit as smooth as possible. On the Continent, André Chapelon had been looking at the steam locomotive's testing and development from a scientific angle. Most advances in locomotive design up to this time had been accomplished through 'trial and error' methods. He carefully analysed the losses in the steam circuits of locomotives and applied proper engineering scrutiny to design improvements to minimise these losses.

Chapelon realised that all parts of the steam circuit were important and paid particular attention to not only getting steam into the cylinders but also out of them. Chapelon decided that the free flowing passage of steam throughout the engine would reduce thermal losses and help to create a higher efficiency. Several of his locomotives had already utilised this idea and were showing high efficiency values and thus savings in fuel. Gresley decided to incorporate this thinking in the new engine and designed all

ABOVE Drawing of smokebox arrangement showing double Kylchap exhaust. *NRM/SSPL*

LEFT Double Kylchap system as installed on No 2001. *NRM/SSPL*

the steam passages through the engine to be as streamlined as possible to avoid any thermal losses and throttling of steam within tight bends in the pipework or castings.

To complement the streamlined passageways Gresley wished to ensure that the steam exhausted the cylinders as cleanly as possible without causing any back pressure. In the early 1930s the double blastpipe arrangement had

become increasingly popular on the Continent with large express passenger engines so equipped hauling prodigious loads with great efficiency. One of the earliest users was the Belgian State Railways (SNCB) who had introduced the system in 1924, again with the aim of reducing back pressure. These engines ran successfully with an increase in power with no discernible side effects or extra running costs. Gresley took an interest in this arrangement and in 1932 wrote to the SNCB and asked for more details with the result that the Belgian Railway sent several drawings. In 1933 Gresley asked his Chief Draughtsman to prepare drawings for this arrangement of double blastpipe for fitting onto his 'A3' Pacifics along with the proposed new 'P2'. However, it seems that Gresley decided not to pursue this system further as, although the work was completed, he never signed off the drawings.

This was not, however, the first time that Gresley had studied the double blastpipe for when he then turned his attention to the Kylala-Chapelon arrangement of double blastpipe and chimney it was not completely new to him as two Class D49 locomotives had been fitted with single-chimney versions in 1929. Chapelon had been witness to the experiments, travelling on one of the engines to comment on the trial

himself. Unfortunately, the tests were deemed to be unsuccessful and the equipment was removed.

On the 'P2', twin exhaust pipes of 6½in diameter entered the smokebox from the cylinder block and into the blastpipe. The blastpipe tops were removable, allowing experimentation to find the most suitable size. Likewise, the blastpipe orifice diameter along with the taper blocks, or vee-bars, could also be changed. The latter divided the exhaust steam as it left the orifice to increase the surface area of the steam to help with draughting. The engine would be built with 5³⁄₁₆in diameter blastpipe orifices and the largest (No 3) size taper blocks, giving a total of 16.4sq in of area for each orifice. After the exhaust steam exited the blastpipe the steam would enter the Kylala spreaders. These tubes were flared at the bottom and then converged onto four further converging vents. These spread the steam further before it entered into two cowls above the spreader then finally entering the two chimney cowls. These cowls initially converged before diverging into the chimney casting and exhausting the steam to atmosphere.

Some engineers may have thought that Gresley's new engine was just a combination of other people's ideas being passed off as his own.

However, Gresley always acknowledged where his ideas and inspiration came from. In his Presidential Address to the Institution of Locomotive Engineers he said: 'The engines of the Paris-Orléans Railway have achieved results in the haulage of long-distance high-speed trains of great weight over a severely graded line which had never been attained by engines of similar size. In preparing the designs of the new eight-wheeled coupled express passenger engine recently constructed at Doncaster, I did not hesitate to incorporate some of the outstanding features of the Paris–Orléans engine, such as the provision of extra large steam passages and a double blast-pipe.'

The boiler was fitted with one live steam injector and unusually, rather than an exhaust steam injector, a boiler feed water and pre-heater equipment. From 1927, 55 'B12s' had been fitted with ACFI (Société l'Auxiliaire des Chemins de Fer et de l'Industrie) feed water heating apparatus. This apparatus was mounted above the boiler and consisted of two heater drums and a single steam cylinder which operated two water pump cylinders. The first of these drew water from the tender into one of the drums where it mixed with exhaust steam. The heated water flowed into the second drum allowing the water to settle and gasses that could be detrimental to boiler life, such as carbon dioxide and oxygen, to vent to atmosphere. From here the second pump drew the pre-heated water into the boiler. All three cylinders were double acting. Darlington Locomotive Works had also equipped a batch of 'C7' class locomotives with ACFI feedwater

heaters before finally equipping two Pacifics – 'A1' No 2576 *The White Knight* and 'A3' No 2580 *Shotover* in August 1929.

Although the feedwater was found to be entering the boiler at high temperature, the maintenance costs of the ACFI apparatus were found to be higher than the savings in fuel. One of the main problems was that the system tended to scale up and required acid cleaning every six weeks. This cleaning in turn tended to damage pipe joints. Eventually the equipment was removed from the various engines, the 'B12s' starting to lose their equipment in 1934 with the last Pacific losing its ACFI gear in 1939. The last ACFI gear in regular use on the LNER was on the Scottish Region-allocated 'B12' engines which

ABOVE 'B12' class No 8507 fitted with ACFI feedwater heating gear stands at Stratford MPD in March 1936. *Steve Armitage Archive*

BELOW J. Richardson (left) and J. Boulby pose for a publicity photograph showing the inside of the cab on *Cock o' the North*. *NRM/SSPL*

lasted until 1941, partially accounted for by the softer water in the region.

With the seeming unsuccessful application of ACFI gear on the LNER it was somewhat surprising that the decision was made to fit the new locomotive with ACFI gear from the outset. On No 2001 the double-acting pump was mounted on the fireman's side of the footplate towards the front of the boiler. The two heater tanks were mounted above the boiler underneath the casing so as not to interrupt the sleek lines of the streamlined body work. Some pipework was mounted beneath a raised cover above the pump on the boiler side. The operating valves were mounted in the cab in place of the usual fireman's-side exhaust steam injector.

The cab layout followed the standard Gresley pattern, with pull-out-style regulator handles on both sides of the cab. The cylinder drain cock handle was fitted on the fireman's side and heat shields fitted to the boiler backhead to protect the locomotive crew from the firebox radiant heat. The driver and fireman were provided with only a basic wooden seat with low cab-side cut-outs. This was soon replaced after the engine entered traffic with padded bucket seats which would also be fitted to the 'A4' class locomotives. High-sided cab cut-outs were also fitted to help reduce draughts for the engineman whilst seated.

Aesthetically, the new engine would look like no other, with a semi-streamlined front end, vee-shaped cab front and unconventional smoke lifting plates. The only locomotive with a passing resemblance was Gresley's experimental 'W1' locomotive. This engine, with its Yarrow water tube boiler, included a fully cased boiler with unconventional front-end appearance.

The 'P2's smokebox front and door sloped backwards at an angle of 12 degrees from vertical whilst the top of the smokebox was set at 15 degrees from horizontal. Behind the double chimney a curved plate was fitted to deflect the flow of air upwards to clear smoke and exhaust steam. The smokebox was surrounded on each side by smoke lifting plates which formed part of the boiler lagging, giving an uninterrupted cladding along the length of the locomotive.

RIGHT The boiler of
No 2001 mounted on the
frames showing AFOL
lagging prior to the
cladding being applied.
NRM/SSPL

Originally the front edges of the smoke deflector plates were set at an angle; the bottoms set directly at the front of the engine whilst the top sloped back to the chimney. However, after wind tunnel testing of a wooden scale model by Dr Dalby at the City & Guilds (Engineering) College, London, it was found that the greatest improvement in deflecting the airflow was created by having vertical fronts to the plates. The same wind tunnel testing was also used to confirm the design of the cab, Gresley having settled on a standard 'A3'-style cab with one improvement, a vee-shaped cab front, which also housed the safety valves in a pocket in the cab roof. The new design reduced the amount of glare in the front spectacle plates when the locomotive was used at night and also helped with the clearance of drifting smoke, both giving great improvements to the driver. This design of cab was later incorporated in all of

Gresley's express passenger locomotives and his 'V2' mixed traffic design.

Again, these designs had been drawn from ideas experienced at home and abroad. Several express passenger engines on the Continent had used vee-shaped cab fronts to help with smoke deflection in the years before No 2001's construction. Interestingly, soon after the construction of the first 'P2', the SNCB railway built a 4-6-2 four-cylinder express locomotive which bore a likeness to 2001. The Belgian engine featured not only a sloped smokebox and vee-shaped cab front but also included ACFI feedwater gear. It seemed that the flow of ideas across the UK and the Continent ran in both directions.

The 'P2' locomotive's boiler was clad in an usual manner, incorporating the previously mentioned deflector plates as part of its sleek design. The cladding also hid the parts of the

LEFT Gresley in the
driver's seat of *Northern
Chief* during the Duke
of York's visit to the
Romney, Hythe &
Dymchurch railway on
5 August 1926. *RH&DR
Association Heritage Group
(Derek Smith collection)*

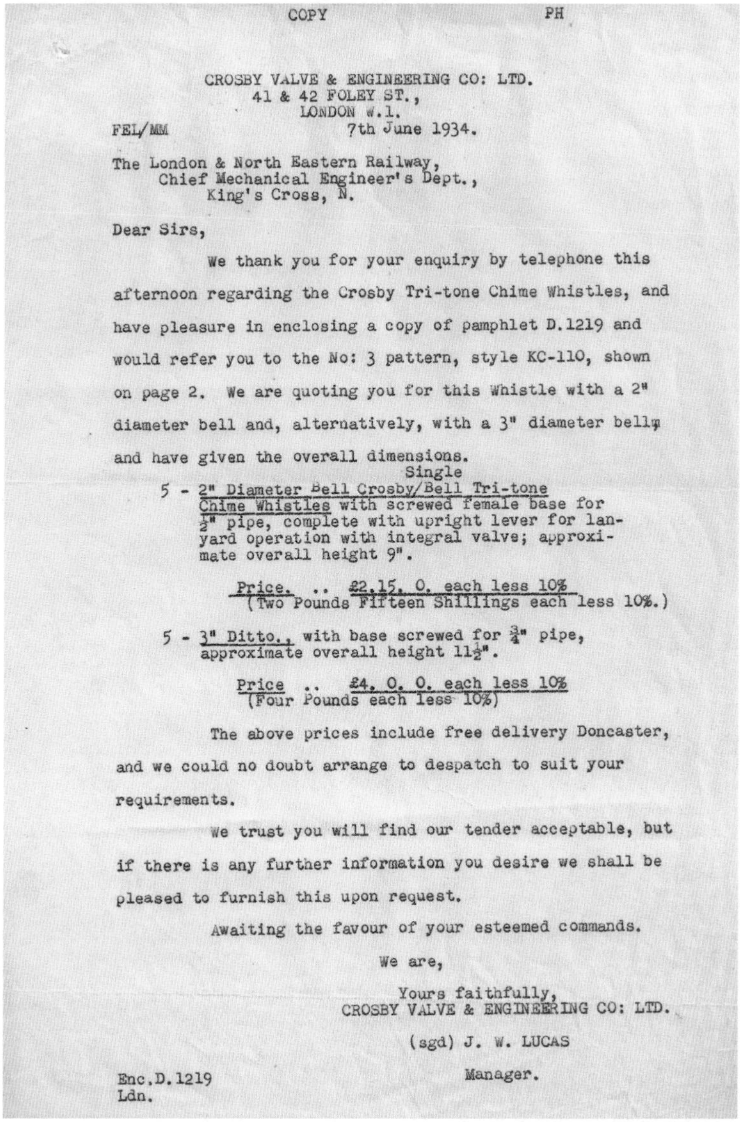

COPY   PH

CROSBY VALVE & ENGINEERING CO: LTD.
41 & 42 FOLEY ST.,
LONDON W.1.
FEL/MM   7th June 1934.

The London & North Eastern Railway,
    Chief Mechanical Engineer's Dept.,
        King's Cross, N.

Dear Sirs,

We thank you for your enquiry by telephone this afternoon regarding the Crosby Tri-tone Chime Whistles, and have pleasure in enclosing a copy of pamphlet D.1219 and would refer you to the No: 3 pattern, style KC-110, shown on page 2. We are quoting you for this Whistle with a 2" diameter bell and, alternatively, with a 3" diameter bell, and have given the overall dimensions.

Single

5 - 2" Diameter Bell Crosby/Bell Tri-tone Chime Whistles with screwed female base for ⅜" pipe, complete with upright lever for lanyard operation with integral valve; approximate overall height 9".

Price. .. £2.15. O. each less 10%
(Two Pounds Fifteen Shillings each less 10%.)

5 - 3" Ditto., with base screwed for ¾" pipe, approximate overall height 11½".

Price .. £4. O. O. each less 10%
(Four Pounds each less 10%)

The above prices include free delivery Doncaster, and we could no doubt arrange to despatch to suit your requirements.

We trust you will find our tender acceptable, but if there is any further information you desire we shall be pleased to furnish this upon request.

Awaiting the favour of your esteemed commands.

We are,

Yours faithfully,
CROSBY VALVE & ENGINEERING CO: LTD.

(sgd) J. W. LUCAS

Manager.

Enc.D.1219
Ldn.

ABOVE Letter to Gresley from the Crosby Valve and Engineering Company quoting for the supply of chime whistles. *NRM/SSPL*

ACFI feedwater equipment and the dome, giving an uninterrupted smooth profile from the cab roof forward to the top of the smokebox. However, under the lagging it was a different story. Once again, Gresley took the opportunity with this new locomotive to experiment with a new form of boiler insulation – Alfol. This insulation, a form of crumpled aluminium foil, gave not only savings in cost but also in weight. The Alfol lagging was used under all the cladding and also between the smoke deflecting plates and the smokebox, allowing the engine's new livery to be applied over all the cladding without the risk of blistering caused by heat.

The locomotive would also be the first in the UK to be fitted with a chime whistle, a feature that would later be found on all of Gresley's Class A4 crack express locomotives. The introduction of the chime whistle to the UK came not via the main line railway companies, but via the privately owned Romney, Hythe & Dymchurch Railway (RHDR). This 15in gauge main line in miniature owned by Captain J. E. P. Howey had been privileged to have a visit from the Duke of York, who on 5 August 1926, drove engine No 2 *Northern Chief* along the railway with Captain Howey squeezed into the small footplate alongside him. Another guest was also present who, like the Duke, enjoyed seeing the locomotives in operation. That person was H. N. Gresley who had developed a friendship with Howey, who had built miniature versions of Gresley's Pacifics to operate on the railway. This friendship led Gresley to arrange for locomotive No 7 *Typhoon* to be displayed next to *Flying Scotsman* at King's Cross for publicity purposes.

Howey was also a fan of the Canadian Pacific Railway and regularly visited to ride on the locomotives. As a result he ordered two locomotives inspired by the Canadian Pacific fleet to become RHDR locomotives, Nos 9 and 10. Shortly after these were built, Captain Howey bought for them two Crosby Chime whistles similar to those used on the full-size locomotives. Soon after No 9 entered traffic, Gresley saw the locomotive, at that time named *Doctor Syn* (now *Winston Churchill*).

Gresley liked the sound of the whistle fitted to locomotive No 9 so much that Captain Howey presented him with the whistle destined for No 10. Gresley did not use the whistle at first and he seems to have kept it as an ornament. However, with the construction of the new express Mikado, Gresley decided to fit the whistle to the new locomotive, specifying it to be fitted 1in in front of and half way up the locomotive chimney. Its prominent position atop the locomotive smokebox in the dead centre of the locomotive helped to enhance and complete the face of his iconic new locomotive and drew much attention in the railway press. Soon after No 2001 was completed Gresley contacted the Crosby Chime

LEFT The completed tender for No 2001 showing the unusual spoked wheels. *NRM/SSPL*

RIGHT The locomotive is lifted ready for wheeling. *NRM/SSPL*

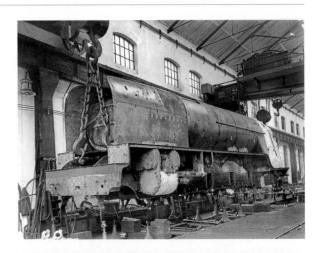

Company and obtained quotes for whistles to equip more LNER express locomotive classes, including the entire fleet of the 'A4s' and later the two streamlined 'B17s', the rebuilt 'W1' and the rest of the 'P2' class. In 1934 Gresley returned the gesture and presented Captain Howey with a chromium-plated 'A4' whistle which is still in use today on the RHDR on locomotive No 8 *Hurricane*, a locomotive based on Gresley's three-cylinder Pacifics.

With so much attention focused on the locomotive it would have been very easy for the LNER to pair the engine with a standard tender; however, the opportunity was again taken to try something new. On 3 March 1933 an order was placed at Doncaster for two 'New Style Non-Corridor' eight-wheel tenders, a design that had appeared in 1930 for a batch of 'A3s'. The order was subsequently reduced to one tender the following month, in accordance with the decision to build only one locomotive. In another departure from normal practice the LNER looked into the feasibility of constructing the tender with an all-welded tender tank. Oliver Bulleid seems to have been the main proponent who saw the advantages of weight saving over the traditional riveted construction.

The LNER had been experimenting with welding on wagons and carriage underframes and was about to transfer to all-welded underframes around this period. However, the company was unsure if it could construct a large welded tender tank in house. Metropolitan-Vickers Electrical Co Ltd at Trafford Park, Manchester, was approached to quote for the construction of either one or two 5,000-gallon welded tender tanks. The following month the firm produced drawings and a quote of £352 for one tank or £644 for two tanks constructed to the specification. Both Bulleid and Gresley examined the drawings and a subsequent order was placed in June for only one tender tank.

The design incorporated a solid baseplate, 24ft 4½in long and 8ft 9in wide. This formed the bottom of the tank and the rear of the footplate. The sides, front and back were then welded in place. The side sheets were 21ft 9in long and incorporated a curved top edge fitted with decorative beading, giving a total height of just over 7ft. These sheets also curved inwards at the front of the tender, bringing the sides in to a distance of 6ft 11in apart, the same distance as the cab side sheets. The coal space sheets, designed with a self-trimming bunker, were constructed separately, again featuring welded construction, before being lifted into place and welded in situ. The design featured the minimum

ABOVE A letter from Gresley discussing the placement of nameplates and the numbers for the new engine. *NRM/SSPL*

amount of material and without rivets a saving of 1 ton 5cwt was made.

However, not all was well with the all-welded construction. Bulleid had arranged for one of the LNER's experienced welding engineers to be present during the tender's construction and report his findings. It seems that some distortion occurred on the large side sheets between the steadying straps. This was noted by the LNER engineer, who on 5 September nonetheless accepted the tank, declaring it satisfactory for use. However, in his report to Bulleid and Gresley after, suggestions were made on how the LNER could improve on the construction and, most importantly, how it could construct the tanks in-house.

The tender was sent to Doncaster to be mated with its chassis, which followed the tried and tested pattern and was mounted on 4ft 2in-diameter wheels. From 1929 onwards all eight-wheeled tenders had been fitted with disc wheels; however, departing from the norm, Gresley instructed the works to procure a set of spoked wheels for the tender on 19 April 1933. No reason was given for this departure from norm and no subsequent eight-wheel tenders were so fitted. The tender body was then fitted-out with handrails, lamp brackets, steps and other fittings as per the Doncaster-built tenders. It was also fitted with two 18in-diameter vacuum cylinders and a vacuum reservoir tank. A water scoop was also fitted between the two inner-most axles with the screw gear and handle mounted on the tender front. The new tender was given the works number 5565 and, unusually, stayed paired with the engine for its entire life, including during two rebuilds and numerous overhauls.

Construction of the locomotive continued at a brisk pace during the early months of 1934. Although Gresley would normally work from his office at King's Cross it was common for him to travel to Doncaster for meetings and to view locomotives under design and construction. This was especially so with the new engine as, although he was happy to

delegate much of the construction to his staff, he wished to be consulted and make all the major decisions. With the engine nearly finished, Gresley sent a letter and a hand-drawn sketch to R. A. Thom (Mechanical Engineer, Doncaster) to show where he wished the nameplate to be fixed on the locomotive. As no locomotive had ever been built with this style, of streamlining apart from the 'W1' (for which 'British Enterprise' nameplates were cast but never actually fitted), Gresley wanted to make sure that the aesthetics of the new locomotive were not spoilt by the 8ft-long nameplate so instructed Thom to have the nameplate temporarily painted on the side of the unfinished locomotive ready for his next visit. The letter also instructed that the number 2001 would be applied to the locomotive and that Gresley had proposed to take the 2001-2010 number range for the 'P2' class rather than the originally assigned number of 2981, which had already been stamped on some of the motion parts.

With the engine mechanically complete, No 2001 was transferred to the Doncaster paintshop for its livery to be applied. As with all the express passenger engines of the time the locomotive was turned out in apple green livery. Boiler bands were painted black with a $\frac{3}{16}$ white edge on either side. The beading around the front of the smoke-lifting plates also received the same treatment. Frames were painted black and included a $\frac{3}{16}$ vermilion line inset by $\frac{1}{2}$in around the outer edge. The cab sides featured a 2in black band across the bottom and a $\frac{1}{2}$in band on the front and back edges, all edged with a thin white line. Lining was even applied to the boiler mudhole doors with a $\frac{1}{2}$in black band with a $\frac{3}{16}$in white line. Handrails were left as burnished steel whilst the wheels were turned out in full apple green livery with a $1\frac{3}{4}$in black rim separated by a white line; similarly, the wheel bosses were painted black and separated again by a white line. The engine's new number, 2001, was applied in 12in gold shaded numerals set 2ft 8in

from the top of the numeral to the bottom of the cab. The tender was treated in a similar fashion with apple green lined with black and white, black frames with red lines and green spoked wheels. 'L.N.E.R.' was also applied in 12in numerals matching the height of the locomotive's number, each being spaced at 3ft 4in intervals.

Finally, a cast brass nameplate was attached to the locomotive. The engine would be the first locomotive to receive a nameplate using the Gill Sans typeface, which had been adopted by the LNER for all its printed material. Although first used on the LNER in 1929 it was not until 1932 that the company reached its aim in unifying all printed material in one typeface. Not missing the opportunity for some publicity, the LNER had asked Eric Gill, the creator of the typeface, to hand paint a *Flying Scotsman* headboard. Gill, who had been a railway enthusiast all his life, was then given the opportunity to ride on the footplate over part of the East Coast Main Line.

The new engine would carry the name *Cock o' the North*, the traditional epithet attached to the head of Clan Gordon in Scotland going back several hundred years. This name was already in use on one of the North British Atlantics working over the route the new engine was destined for. With No 2001 assuming the name, the Atlantic was renamed *Aberdonian*, taking its name from a withdrawn member of the class.

The engine now complete, it emerged from the paintshop in time for its official works photographs before being hastily added to the line-up of displays at Doncaster Works open day on 26 and 27 May 1934. A total of 39,352 people, including some 4,000 schoolchildren, attended the event which featured not only the brand new Mikado but also *Flying Scotsman* and the LNER Garratt heavy freight engine. Just a few days later on 1 June the engine would be unveiled to the world at a special press launch at King's Cross.

ABOVE Staff, including (from left to right) R. A. Thom, E. Windle, J. S. Jones, J. Eggleshaw, two chargehand fitters, erecting shop foreman and paintshop foreman, pose with the finished engine in May 1934. *NRM/SSPL*

RIGHT The completed engine on display at Doncaster Works open day, 26 May 1934. *P2SLC Collection*

CHAPTER 3

TESTING TIMES

On 31 May 1934 *Cock o' the North* left the plant ready to run to London prior to its unveiling to the public the following day. The engine was displayed at King's Cross station during the morning whilst official photographs were taken before a run for the news services and press reporters in the afternoon. Few details of this run have been found but it seems likely that the train worked from King's Cross to Peterborough or Barkston and return. Gresley was present for the event overseeing the stage management of the event carefully.

The following day the engine was taken to Ilford via the Great Eastern lines to appear at an LNER rolling stock exhibition. The event was the first to openly advertise the display of a 'P2' locomotive and drew nearly 30,000 paying people, raising over £750 for local charities. The event also featured 'A3' *Flying Scotsman* along with a 'B12/3', *Claud Hamilton*, 'B17' *Sandringham* and a small group of shunting locomotives. The event also included music by the local LNER band and, interestingly, was the first to use the local steam brakedown crane to give rides to members of the public for 2d for adults and 1d for children, who were hoisted into the air in a wagon body, something which later became a regular attraction at LNER open days.

On 3 June the engine was once again on its travels, this time light engine to Edinburgh via the East Coast Main Line. This move was in anticipation of a special train over the 130 miles from Edinburgh to Aberdeen, the first time that the engine would work the route it was designed for. The train was formed of 12 carriages and carried a small group of dignitaries and invited guests including Sir Nigel Gresley. Very few details of this run have survived but it seems to have been satisfactory. The engine stabled overnight at Aberdeen Ferryhill ready for a display at Aberdeen station the following day. During this event Gresley gave the Lord Provost a guided tour of the locomotive. The public were then admitted to the display between 10.30 and 12.30 when several hundred people came to see it. After the display, in the early afternoon the engine and Gresley once again returned to Edinburgh, the locomotive spending the night at Haymarket before going on display at Edinburgh Waverley the following day. Again Gresley gave the local Lord Provost of Edinburgh a personal tour and explanation of the engine before the general public were admitted. The engine then returned south, eventually arriving sometime before 9 June, when the engine was sent specially to King's Cross so that the BBC

could interview the driver about the locomotive for the programme *In Town Tonight*. Unfortunately, as far as the author is aware, the original recording that included the engine's chime whistle being blown has not survived although it is known that Driver G. Trower was interviewed by Frank Giles, a 13-year-old autograph hunter, as part of the recording.

The engine, which by now had already accrued several hundred miles of running in, was given some regular work in readiness for serious testing. However, this work was not in Scotland where the engine was designed to operate but on the Southern section of the ECML working from King's Cross Top Shed. From 11 to 18 June 1934 the engine worked the 10.50am service from King's Cross to Peterborough, leaving at 14.28 on the return leg. This train, locally known as the 'Parly', was entrusted to the King's Cross driver C. Peachy. The engine worked the train on all the dates with the exception of the 17 when it was stopped for routine examination. On the 14th Bulleid rode on the engine's footplate to witness its performance, afterwards remarking that its performance was 'really extraordinarily good'.

On 19 July *Cock o' the North* was given its first opportunity to prove itself on a special test train

from King's Cross to Barkston and back again under the command of Driver Peachy who had by now become quite familiar with the engine. The train was formed of 19 vehicles including the ex-NER dynamometer, car giving a total train weight of 649 tons. Leaving King's Cross, the engine started the train with ease giving an initial drawbar pull of 14 tons. Within 750yds the cut-off was reduced to 45% and the speed increased to 20mph whilst travelling up the 1 in 105 climb. At the two-mile mark speed had risen to 32.5mph. After four miles the engine was running at 58mph and started the steady eight-mile climb of 1 in 200. At this point the pull on the drawbar had reached 15 tons, the equivalent to 1,730 drawbar horsepower (dbhp) at a cut-off of 20%. This was lengthened to 25% half-way up the bank and the engine performed well with the boiler pressure never falling below 195psi and the train reaching the summit at 50.5mph. The train then continued to Hatfield, the first timing point, and was passed at 70mph 22½ minutes after leaving King's Cross, the usual time allowed for an express train on this section being 26 minutes. Nothing special happened between Hatfield and Hitchin, the engine running 30 seconds under the booked time with a calculated figure of 1,300dbhp. Again, the run to Huntingdon was light and the

ABOVE *Cock o' the North* is readied for its inaugural run for the press on 1 June 1934. *P2SLC Collection*

RIGHT *Cock o' the North* stands next to 'A3' No 4479 *Robert the Devil* during the King's Cross launch. *Rail Archive Stephenson*

RIGHT *Cock o' the North* is turned on the turntable at King's Cross ready for its launch on 1 June 1934. Sir Nigel Gresley, complete with cigar, watches on. *Ian MacCabe Collection*

TOP LEFT Gresley shows the Lord Provost the locomotive's unique front end streamlining at Aberdeen station on 4 June 1934. *P2SLC Collection*

CENTRE LEFT No 2001 stands at the buffer stops, unusually facing north ready for the radio

broadcast of 'In Town Tonight'. *Ian MacCabe Collection*

BOTTOM LEFT *Cock o' the North* complete with indicator shelter and dynamometer car leaves King's Cross on an early test run in June 1934. *P2SLC Collection*

driver took the opportunity to pull the engine up to 10% cut-off and the engine continued to run at a sustained 70mph. After Huntingdon the line climbs at 1 in 200 for three miles and the engine's cut-off was increased to 15%, allowing its speed to reach 53mph at the peak of the climb. Speed restrictions meant an interrupted run into Peterborough, where the engine paused. Starting away, a drawbar pull of 16 ½ tons was measured, falling to 12 tons as the speed rose to 10mph. Driver Peachey slowly notched the engine up until the 20% cut off was reached at 33mph. Speed increased and during the two miles of 1 in 264 near Essendine the speed did not fall below 60mph. The next sustained five-mile climb of 1 in 200 at Little Bytham was taken at 20% cut-off with 1,700 drawbar horsepower being recorded at 58mph before the reverser was let out to 25% and the horsepower increased to 1,800 at 56mph. During the climb the boiler pressure was sustained between 210 and 215psi. As the engine reached the top of the bank, the driver was instructed to increase the cut-off to 30%. On this level section the engine reached a speed of 57½mph and 6.1 tons was recorded on the drawbar by the dynamometer car, giving a drawbar horsepower of 2,100. Reaching Corby, the railway again climbs for three miles at 1 in 178. With the reverser set at 30% the engine started up the bank at 60mph losing little speed during the climb. Grantham was reached two and a half minutes quicker than the booked 34½half minutes allowed. The short journey on to Barkston on the falling gradients was steady and uneventful.

Once the engine reached its destination the entire train was turned on the Barkston triangle and the engine examined ready for its return trip. The return run was for the most part uneventful with the highest drawbar horsepower being 2,100 horsepower on the 1 in 200 climb south of Hitchin, again tackled with the reverser at 30% cut-off and a speed of 60mph. Passing New Barnet, the highest speed during the test of

76mph was achieved, at which point the regulator was closed and the engine placed in mid-gear, coasting nearly all the way to the buffer stops at King's Cross and arriving a few minutes early. The tests were widely reported in the railway press and it was declared that the engine's performance on the uphill sections beat every record held previously on the LNER main line.

However, it was not just the railway press that had shown an interest in the new LNER locomotive. The engine was such a departure from the norm that the general public became fascinated with the locomotive and the LNER Advertising Department made the most of it. The company offered a pewter model and sectional drawing of the locomotive for sale at its exhibitions and via its agency. News of the locomotive soon spread in conjunction with its early exhibitions. Soon local and national newspapers were carrying news of the engine's introduction to service, testing and appearance across the LNER system. The news was not just confined to the UK as the *Montreal Gazette* in Canada on 22 June 1934 and the *Pittsburgh Press* in the USA on 1 July both reported on the completion of the new locomotive.

The engine spurred the public's imagination and several firms in conjunction with the LNER offered cigarette cards, cardboard cut-outs, badges and even plans for large-scale fret-saw model projects for sale. One entrepreneurial sweet shop owner in Dundee had a 3ft-long chocolate model of the new engine constructed for the shop window, which itself was reported in the local newspaper. The engine had become famous in its own right and even found its way onto the silver screen in the aptly named film *Cock o' the North*. The film was directed by Oswald Mitchell and starred George Carney, Marie Lohr and Ronnie Hepworth and told the story of an engine driver who was forced into

BELOW A wooden studio mock up of No 2001's cab, built from works drawings in May 1935, for the feature film *'Cock o' the North'*. Driver Glasgow (far right) is seen offering advice to actor George Carney. *Ian MacCabe Collection*

ABOVE No 2001 heads a heavy 649-ton test train past Welwyn on 19 June 1934. *P2SLC Collection*

"COCK O' THE NORTH" IN CHOCOLATE.

A chocolate model of the L.N.E.R. Company's latest super-locomotive, "Cock o' the North," has been placed in the shop window at 68 High Street, Dundee, of James Keiller & Son, Ltd.

Nearly four feet in length, the model is made exactly to scale, and reproduces faithfully the huge boiler and diminutive funnel of the engine. An engine-driver dressed as Santa Claus is peeping from the cabin, while the tender is packed with chocolates instead of coals.

LEFT Newspaper cutting from the *Dundee Courier*, Wednesday, 5 December 1934. *P2SLC Collection*

RIGHT *Cock o' the North* at Ilford LNER exhibition in company with No 4472 *Flying Scotsman*.
P2SLC Collection

RIGHT Whilst No 2001 was on display at Ilford the LNER publicity department took the opportunity to sell pewter models of the new locomotive.
P2SLC Collection

BELOW One of the original LNER paperweights produced by the LNER Advertising Department.
Graeme Bunker

retirement following an accident and who found consolation in his son. For some scenes in the film full-size mock of No 2001's cab and tender front was built in the film studios from drawings supplied by the LNER Advertising Department, who also arranged for the company to film the engine whilst it was at work around King's Cross.

The engine, however, had returned immediately from its 19 July test run to continue work on the 'Parly' trains, now in the hands of Driver W. A. Sparshatt, another Top Link man from King's Cross Top Shed. In the hands of Sparshatt the engine put in some fast runs, arriving early at its destination on every occasion that week. On 21 June the engine was working the 1.30pm train from King's Cross and reached a top speed of 83mph on several occasions before reaching

Peterborough three minutes early despite a severe permanent way restriction at Yaxley.

Further dynamometer car tests were carried out, firstly with an uneventful run on 27 June before several trips during the first week of July. The July trains were also used to take indicator readings from the cylinders and were worked from Doncaster, usually on the 11.40am departure from Doncaster of about 420 tons and a return working at 4pm with a train of around 580 tons to Peterborough, then reduced to 420 tons onwards to Doncaster.

The first of these runs took place on 2 July and it seems that the fireman on the outward trip had problems maintaining steam pressure. Leaving Doncaster the pressure was down to 180psi and during the trip low pressures were also recorded at Tuxford (this location is between Retford and Newark and mentioned in official notes), Newark, Barkston, Grantham and Corby. During this run the ACFI feedwater heater also gave trouble and the fireman had to rely on the one live steam injector. The driver worked the engine as far as Peterborough with a continuously fully opened regulator and only closed it for restrictions and before braking was required. When the train reached the summit of Stoke Bank the engine was allowed to accelerate until a maximum speed of 87½mph was reached, during which the engine was running at 12% cut-off and the regulator left wide open until six miles after the summit had passed. All of these events were recorded on the dynamometer rolls and when the train reached

King's Cross Gresley came down from his office above the station to examine them. On realising that the engine had reached such a high speed he immediately issued the instruction to the engineer in charge of the test that this was not to happen again and that the engine was to go fast up and coast down the banks.

During the same tests the following day it seems that Gresley's instructions were adhered to. Running down Stoke Bank the engine reached a top speed of 71mph before being allowed to slow to 64mph towards Essendine, at which point the engine was once again given power and allowed to run up to 69mph at Werrington water troughs where the brakes were applied ready for the stop at Peterborough. Leaving Peterborough,

ABOVE No 2001, equipped with indicator shelter as part of its testing, stands at King's Cross being prepared for its next test run. *NRM/SSPL*

BELOW No 2001 heads the 5:45pm King's Cross to Leeds express out of Hadley Wood North Tunnel. May 1935. *Frank R. Hebron – Rail Archive Stephenson*

the engine worked up to a maximum speed of 72mph on two occasions, firstly at Tempsford and then again at New Barnet. At the latter the engine was once again shut off and allowed to coast the nine miles to King's Cross. On this journey the fireman had no issues producing steam with the gauge rarely showing anything below 200psi. The return working, however, did not run so well. Leaving King's Cross and entering Copenhagen Tunnel the engine primed badly covering the dynamometer car and first few passenger carriages with water and grime from the tunnel along with causing some damage to the tunnel lining. The test engineers decided that the blast was too heavy and once again the engine was returned to the works to have the blastpipe tops opened out to 5½inches whilst retaining the No 3 taper blocks. The resulting work meant that the planned tests on 4 July were cancelled until the modifications (and cleaning the dynamometer car) were completed. However, tests were resumed on 5 July, this time with the aim of taking indicator readings of the cylinders

when working at 15% cut-off to investigate the cylinder compression pressures. Unfortunately, on the run to King's Cross the engine's right-hand side gudgeon pin overheated and the engine was pronounced a failure and was replaced by another locomotive for the return working whilst the engine received attention at King's Cross shed.

The following week the engine returned to testing with the dynamometer car with a trip from Doncaster to King's Cross on 10 July and a return trip from King's Cross to Grantham on the 11th. For these trips the taper blocks had been changed to the smaller No 1 size. On both these trips the engine had further steaming problems. On the Grantham train the return leg left at 5.44pm and although the boiler pressure started at 200psi it rapidly fell to 165psi whilst passing Stoke signal box. However, down Stoke bank the engine soon recovered and a speed of 73½mph was reached before the stop at Peterborough. After the stop, the engine seemed in better shape with a fast run to Tempsford where a maximum speed of 76½mph was reached, recovering two minutes of lost time before arriving at King's Cross.

Whilst on test it was found that the sine wave superheat elements were prone to rapid erosion and it was decided that they should be removed even though the tests had shown that a temperature of 750 degrees Fahrenheit could be obtained, a temperature far higher than obtainable in the 'A3s' at the time. In July 1934 these elements were removed and replaced by a new Robinson superheater with 10ft 6in elements. These elements stretched almost the entire length of the flue tubes, stopping only 9in short of the firebox tubeplate. These new elements increased the heating surface to 776.5sq.ft. Whilst on test later at Vitry the new superheater elements produced a steam temperature of 765 degrees Fahrenheit.

With the dynamometer car testing completed, the engine was allowed to run a series of four test runs without the car solely for the purpose of experimenting with the combinations of blastpipe tops and taper blocks and the inclusion (or exclusion) of Kylchap cowls. On 13 July the first run took place, the engine fitted with 5½in-diameter blastpipe tops and No 1 taper blocks and no cowls. The engineers involved in the test recorded that this set-up would adequately meet any conditions required whilst the engine was operating on the Southern Area of the LNER. The next day the blastpipe top was increased to 5¾in and the taper blocks removed completely. On this test it was found that the engine would not steam when running with short cut-offs unless the regulator was wide open. The following day the same test was carried out but with a No 3 taper block fitted. This once again produced good results and was approved by the engineers for running on the Southern Area. Finally, on 16 July the engine had its Kylchap cowls refitted and again undertook the same testing. In this configuration the engine performed faultlessly with ample reserve spare, leading to the engineers suggesting that this configuration be kept and that it was considered capable of covering any condition as required in the Scottish Area.

It was in this condition that the engine was sent to Scotland on 30 July 1934 and allocated to Haymarket shed, ready to start the regular

working on the type of trains that the engine was designed for. The engine originally worked trains over the entire length of the route from Edinburgh to Aberdeen and very quickly earned the nickname 'The Miners Friend' on account of its heavy coal consumption. During these early days the engine had its own regular driver, D. McGuire, a senior man in the No 2 Link which was locally known as 'The Dundees'. On 1 and 2 August the engine was submitted to test runs from Edinburgh to Aberdeen and back on a 586-ton train. Coal consumption was reported to be high enough to worry the local Inspectors and Scottish Area managers and subsequently the engine was only

TOP No 2001 rounds the curve on the climb out of Inverkeithing with the 2pm Edinburgh to Aberdeen express. *NRM/SSPL*

ABOVE *Cock o' the North* is prepared at Edinburgh Haymarket Depot ready to work the 'Aberdonian'. *Transport Treasury*

THE "SILVER LINK" SILVER JUBILEE CLASS, No. 5645

RAILWAY EXHIBITION

OF THE LATEST

LOCOMOTIVES, CARRIAGES

AND OTHER VEHICLES

IN AID OF

Aberdeen Royal Infirmary Building Fund

ABERDEEN JOINT STATION

SATURDAY, 14th NOVEMBER, 1936—10.0 a.m. to 10.0 p.m.
SUNDAY, 15th November, 1936—2.0 p.m. to 10.0 p.m.

PROGRAMME — PRICE ONE PENNY

THE "PRINCESS ELIZABETH" THE "COCK O' THE NORTH"

Henry Munro, Ltd., Union Row, Aberdeen.

SPLENDID **FREE GIFT** WITHIN!

The **MODERN BOY**

EVERY SATURDAY WEEK ENDING SEP. 29 1934 No. 347 VOL. 14 **2**d

MAGNIFICENT **METAL MODEL** OF THE **L.N.E.R.** CRACK EXPRESS ENGINE "COCK O' THE NORTH" IN FULL COLOURS **FREE** INSIDE!

Next Week—The latest L.M.S. loco 'Princess Royal!'

used over part of the journey from Edinburgh to Dundee, usually on the 2pm from Waverley returning from Dundee at 5.40pm. There is no contemporary evidence that the engine ever ran out of coal on normal service trains but it is recorded that on more than one occasion the engine arrived with very little in reserve.

However, the engine was soon returned to Doncaster, hauling the 11.30am parcels train from Edinburgh on 23 August, so that two new scroll cams could be fitted. On removal, it was noticed that the cams were damaged, showing signs of pitting and grooving, and the cam rollers were also deformed. The decision was made to equip the engine with stepped cams and an order was placed with the manufacturers to supply a set for the engine. With the work complete the engine

was returned to Scotland and again took up work on the Edinburgh to Dundee trains it had previously worked. The engine continued this work for several weeks before again returning to Doncaster on 9 September to have a new left-hand piston fitted, returning to Scotland on the 16.

It seems that Gresley and Bulleid were concerned about the coal consumption of the engine and so *Cock o' the North* was subjected to coal consumption tests between Edinburgh and Dundee on 1 October. Teddy Windle, Doncaster's Chief Draughtsman, travelled to Edinburgh to ride on the locomotive and oversee the tests along with J. Bartholomew, the Chief Locomotive Inspector for the Scottish Area, whilst the engine was driven throughout by its regular driver. In the usual manner for these tests only the minimum amount of coal deemed necessary for the journey was placed in the tender with a further quantity of weighed coal kept in reserve in bags stowed at the back of the tender. Unfortunately, it seems that a combination of

ABOVE *Cock o' the North* departs from Edinburgh Waverley with the 9.55am express for Aberdeen in August 1935. *Rail Archive Stephenson*

the under-estimation of the required amount of coal coupled with the heavy-handed driving (apparently a regular occurrence with Driver McGuire, even in the presence of an Inspector) resulted in the locomotive running out of coal at Dalmeny on the return journey. Coal was obtained from the signal box bunker which allowed the locomotive to continue to Edinburgh with a delay to the passenger train of some 45 minutes on arrival at Waverley.

After some consideration the test was repeated on 6 October, working the 2pm Edinburgh to Aberdeen train as far as Dundee and then returning from Dundee at 5.40pm. For this test the engine had its blastpipe top changed for a 6in-diameter fitting. On the return portion the

LEFT No 2001 crosses
the Forth Bridge with
a heavy express service.
P2SLC Collection

load was 543 tons as far as Thornton where the Glasgow coaches were detached, decreasing the weight to 465 tons. It was reported that the fireman had difficulty in maintaining the boiler pressure with several occurrences of the needle falling to 180psi. However, whenever the regulator was shut for restrictions or for breaking the pressure soon recovered. On the round trip from Edinburgh the total amount of coal consumed was 5 tons 9cwt giving a consumption of 103.75lb per train mile. This was adjusted to factor out the fuel used while the engine was on layover at Dundee to 91.9lb per engine mile – still a high figure. Shortly after these tests the engine returned to Doncaster for attention.

Gresley consulted Chapelon about the engine and mentioned that the locomotive steamed properly with the 6in blastpipe top and small taper blocks. This surprised Chapelon as it would have made the cross-sectional area through which the steam passed far larger than the French practice to obtain perfect results of evaporation and as such the engine would suffer from reduced power in

some circumstances. Chapelon suggested reverting to the smaller blastpipe top so that the engine could develop its potential power at all times. However, Gresley disagreed and arranged for the engine to undertake a week of tests monitoring the smokebox vacuum during different working conditions with the engine's blastpipe apparatus still with the 6in tops. During one of these tests it is recorded that the engine achieved a speed of 80mph under the control of Driver W. Sowden. The tests continued into the following week with the engine handed over to Driver G. Trower of Doncaster, who had been selected to undertake testing of the locomotive on its forthcoming trip to France. On the penultimate day of testing the taper blocks were removed completely and on the final day a new blastpipe top of 5⅞in was fitted to the engine. Steaming continued to be good but at the end of the testing it was found that the engine's left-hand connecting rod had run hot. The engine was subsequently sent to the plant for more sideplay to be provided in the connecting rod bushes and preparations made for its foreign adventure.

CHAPTER 4

MIKADO EVOLUTION

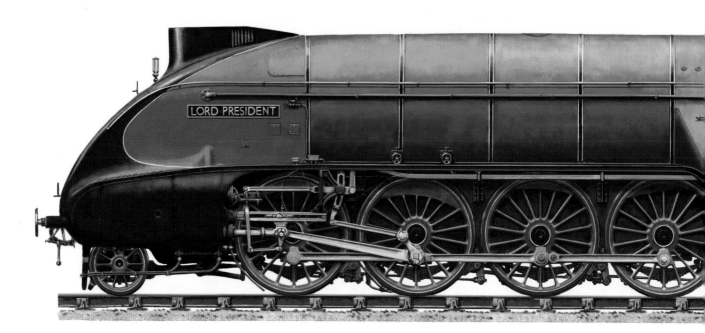

Cock o' the North was not destined to be the sole member of the 'P2' family. In November 1933 the LNER board authorised the construction of a further five 'P2' class locomotives along with a batch of 'A3' and 'V1'-type engines. However, the decision was soon made to complete just one engine, reserving the construction of the following four until trials with the next locomotive, destined to become No 2002, were completed. The basis of the new locomotive was similar to the first example; however, the outline diagram produced the month before the construction order was given showed two notable differences. Firstly, the Lentz rotary valve gear had been replaced by the more traditional Walschaerts valve gear and piston valves with the inside cylinder driven by the tried and tested Gresley conjugated 2 to 1 link motion. The other noticeable difference was the inclusion of a single chimney. Gresley soon decided that he wanted the new engine to be nearly identical to the first engine with the exception of the Lentz valve gear and cylinders, which meant amending the design to keep the Kylchap arrangement of double chimney. The cylinder block was once again of a monobloc construction and featured 9in piston valves which meant that the cylinder clearance volumes were

dramatically reduced compared to No 2001, being around 7.5%. As the design developed, and with the hindsight of *Cock o' the North*'s introduction in June 1934, it was decided to omit the ACFI feed water heater and fit an exhaust steam injector. All the differences meant that the locomotive's weight differed from its counterpart with the new engine weighing in at 109 tons 8cwt rather than the 110 tons 5cwt of No 2001. The engine was coupled to a 'new-type non-corridor tender' similar to *Cock o' the North*'s except that this tender was fabricated in the traditional riveted manner and sat on the regular LNER-pattern solid-centre disc wheels. In total, the tender weighed more than No 2001's, at 57 tons 18cwt.

The new engine was given the name *Earl Marischal*, the hereditary title of the Keith family. It is interesting to note that Dunnottar Castle, the family seat, was visible from the Aberdeen main line near Stonehaven. The engine left the works on 6 October 1934 and, like its predecessor, started a series of tests and running in on the Southern section of the East Coast Main Line.

With the engine complete it was displayed at York station for one of the LNER's open days in company with No 10000 'Hush Hush' and various other exhibits before setting about running-in

trials and testing and spending an extended period based at Doncaster shed. Once again the Engineers at Doncaster paid particular attention to the blastpipe tops and taper blocks. As outshopped, the engine was equipped with 5⅞in-diameter blastpipe tops and No 3 taper blocks. On 12 December 1934 observations were made and recorded with the engine working the 12.20pm Doncaster to King's Cross service. The up train was formed of nine vehicles weighing 232 tons, this being increased at Retford and Grantham until a final train weight of 341 tons was formed, a load well within the capability of the 'P2'. However, although the engine kept to booked time, it was noted that full boiler pressure was only achieved during the station stops. Whilst running, the pressure quickly fell away to 175psi or less. The return journey from King's Cross was formed of a 400-ton train of 12 vehicles on a semi-fast express. Once again the engine struggled to maintain boiler pressure, with the climb of Stoke bank being particularly difficult, resulting in the exhaust steam injector being shut off and the blower turned well up to aid steaming. During both journeys it was noticed that there was little draw on the fire and no sparks were noted being thrown from the chimney, leading to the conclusion that

there was insufficient draughting on the fire. The following month the engine was fitted with 5¾in diameter blastpipe tops, whilst retaining the same sized taper blocks, before being tested on 24 January on the same Doncaster to London and return train. On this occasion observations were only made on the return journey, once again formed of 12 vehicles weighing 400 tons. The new blastpipe top arrangement produced far better results with the fireman holding the pressure steady between the 200-215psi marks for nearly the entire journey. Only on one occasion, near the summit of Stoke bank, did the pressure fall dramatically to 165psi, resulting in the cut-off, which had previously been at 15% for the ascent of the bank, being let out to 25%. Although the engine lost 1 minute on its booked time between Peterborough and Grantham the modification was considered a success with the fire being drawn much brighter and better steaming results. This modification would later be incorporated into the other members of the 'P2' class.

During the same period, however, it was noted that the engine suffered from drifting smoke and exhaust steam obscuring the driver's forward vision, particularly when the engine was being worked at shorter cut-offs. It seemed that

the semi-streamlined front end was not as effective in lifting the smoke and steam when combined with the engine's arrangement of Walschaerts gear and piston valves. This arrangement did not produce the crisp exhaust that was so prominent on *Cock o' the North*. Gresley once again turned to City & Guilds (Engineering) College which set about conducting scale model wind tunnel testing. After some experimentation it was decided that additional smoke lifting plates were required and these were fitted during April 1935. These plates were placed outside the original smoke lifting sheets and featured a slight curve, resulting in the bottom spaced 1ft 5⅛in away from the originals at the bottom, tapering to 6in distance at the top. At the time of fitting the original smoke lifting sheets had their decorative beading removed and the boiler handrails were cut back to follow suit. The nameplates were also transferred from the original cladding to the new deflectors, now sitting 7¼in lower than previously, so that they would not foul the curved section. Finally, small upward curving plates were fitted behind the new smoke lifting plates to aid the direction of air upwards clear of the engine. When the engine re-entered service the additional sheets solved the previous problems of smoke drifting. Unfortunately, the aesthetic appearance of the engine suffered, with the sleek lines of the semi streamlined front end lost behind the sheets, leading to the unfortunate nickname 'big ears'.

Like its relative, *Earl Marischal* attracted considerable interest from the press and railway enthusiasts alike. One of the earliest accounts of the engine was recorded in the January 1935 issue of *The Railway Magazine* by Cecil J. Allen who, by good fortune, stumbled across the engine on a wet and foggy December day in 1934 working the 4pm train from King's Cross to Doncaster. The train consisted of 17 vehicles including two heavy eight-wheeled dining cars,

ABOVE *Earl Marischal* freshly outshopped from Doncaster Works. *NRM/SSPL*

BELOW No 2002 receives attention from its driver whilst at King's Cross shed during its running-in period. *P2SLC Collection*

RIGHT To advertise the development of East Coast Main Line express locomotives the LNER staged a parallel run of an Ivatt Atlantic, Gresley 'A3' and a brand new 'P2', No 2002. *Ian Allan Library*

one buffet car, a twin articulated set along with a six-wheeled van directly behind the engine, undertaking funerary purposes, giving a gross load of 580 tons. Allen remarked that 'it was clearly evident, however, that the driver had no intention of imitating the speed of a hearse'. Leaving the terminus, the engine lifted the heavy train with ease, passing Finsbury Park in less than six minutes before passing Stroud Green at 52mph. Some slow running occurred before Potters Bar then the engine was really allowed to get into its stride, passing Hitchin at 70mph and hitting a top speed of 79mph at Arlesey. Until the next stop, speed was often in the mid 70s with the engine seemingly at ease with its heavy train. Arriving at Peterborough 5 minutes early the engine took a short break awaiting a connecting train and portions of the train were removed. Leaving Peterborough, the train weighed 400 tons and within the eight miles to Tallington the engine reached 68mph before climbing up the 1 in 200 climb at Corby at a minimum of 54mph and the 1 in 178 of Stoke Summit at 50mph then a dash of low 70mph running to its stop at Grantham. Leaving Grantham, the 14.6 miles to Newark were covered in 15.54 minutes, a minute faster than the allowed time, with a top speed of 77.5mph reached at Claypole. After Newark the engine accelerated into the mid 70s once again, arriving at Retford several minutes before the

THE EARL MARISCHAL
L.N.E.R.

TOP *Earl Marischal*, without its extra smoke deflectors, running at speed on an East Coast Main Line express.
P2SLC Collection

ABOVE Contemporary cigarette card showing the new *Earl Marischal*.
P2SLC Collection

TOP No 2002 leaving Hadley Wood North Tunnel with the 4pm King's Cross to Leeds express during May 1935. *Rail Archive Stephenson*

ABOVE Works photograph of *Earl Marischal* fitted with additional smoke-lifting plates. *NRM/SSPL*

booked time. The last section to Doncaster occurred in thick fog and the engine's driver took it steady due to the conditions but still arrived a few seconds before the booked time. Summing up the account, Allen concluded that the engine gained over 12 minutes on the journey and gave 'an impressive demonstration of possibilities in ordinary service'.

Whilst the engine was based at Doncaster it was employed on one of two different Doncaster to London King's Cross diagrams, arriving at the London terminus at either 1.55pm or 3.55pm and departing the capital at either 4pm or 5.45pm. For a brief period during April and May 1935 when both *Cock o' the North* and *Earl Marischal* were available and operating from Doncaster, both turns would be covered by the engines, allowing the public the opportunity to see both of the LNER's unique express Mikados at King's Cross. This working however would finish on 22 May when No 2002 left on the 4pm train, followed by No 2001 leaving on the 5.45pm train to Doncaster, both engines leaving London for the last time. On arrival at Doncaster both engines entered the plant for final work before being permanently transferred to Scotland in June 1935.

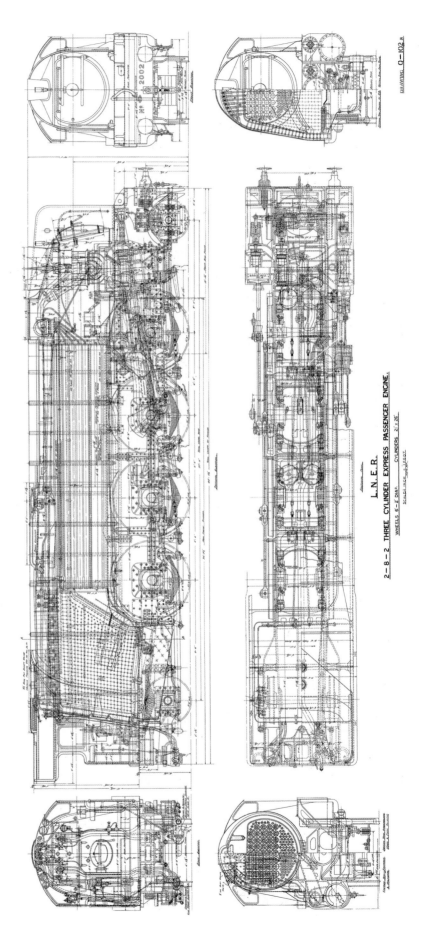

ABOVE No 2002 stands at Dundee Tay Bridge shed coaling stage. *P2SLC Collection*

RIGHT *Earl Marischal* heads a heavy passenger working at Montrose station. Rather than remove the headboard completely it was common for crews to just reverse the 'Aberdonian' headboard when returning on a normal working. *P2SLC Collection*

LEFT General Arrangement of No 2002. *NRM/SSPL*

CHAPTER 5

THE LNER AMBASSADOR

Gresley had first expressed interest in a locomotive testing plant in 1927 and used his Presidential Address to the Institute of Locomotive Engineers to advocate the building of a national 'locomotive experimental station', not only for the use of the Big Four companies but also for the private manufacturers, for all of whom testing in a scientific manner of a locomotive and its sub assemblies would be of great benefit. At the time the only testing facility in the UK was a small facility inside the Swindon works of the GWR; however, this was not big enough for many of the larger express passenger and freight locomotives then being built. The Government later adopted the plan and a committee was set up to examine the proposal. The report in June 1930 recommended that such a facility should be built but the economic situation of the early 1930s caused the report to be shelved and nothing was moved forward, much to Gresley's frustration. However, a similar idea had been developed in France, and in 1933 a locomotive testing plant was opened in Vitry-sur-Seine near Paris, funded entirely by the French Government. Gresley was present at the opening ceremony and was greatly impressed by the facilities.

Due to this lack of a suitable testing station in the UK, one of Gresley's French counterparts, André Chapelon, arranged a visit for *Cock o' the North* to the newly opened locomotive test bed at Vitry the following year. The pair had first met whilst Chapelon was in the UK in 1926 visiting Davey Paxman, at the time the licence holder for the Lentz poppet valves and associated gear in Western Europe. Gresley had already started experimenting with the Lentz gear on several locomotives and it seems that the technical director at Paxman arranged for the pair to meet at their works in Colchester to discuss the valves and their uses. From this early meeting a fruitful friendship blossomed with Chapelon and Gresley sharing ideas and theories with each other.

Cock o' the North had already undergone a series of tests based out of Doncaster and King's Cross hauling various trains whilst equipped with an indicator shelter. Prior to leaving for the Continent the locomotive was returned to Doncaster and entered the paint shop to be touched up alongside three 40-ton bogie coal wagons which were also painted with 'London & North Eastern Railway Best Yorkshire Coal Yorkshire Main Colliery' on their sides. These

vehicles, along with a standard type box van containing lubricating oil, spare parts including axleboxes, coupling rod brasses, gauge glasses and other consumables, and a 20-ton brakevan formed the train that left Doncaster bound for Harwich and the Continent. The engine also had some minor work to ensure that the tests in France were as accurate as possible, including the tyres being turned to ensure they were within a 0.5mm accuracy, and adjustment to the horn blocks to ensure that the axles were perfectly parallel. The locomotive also had stepped cams fitted in place of the infinitely variable cams. These stepped cams had six cut-off positions: 12, 18, 25, 35, 45 and 75% in forward gear whilst the reverse gear had only two settings, 35 and 75%. At this time the maximum cut-off was increased from 70%, as on the originally fitted scroll cams, to 75% to aid the starting of heavier trains.

The poppet valves were reground along with the safety valves, and other gauges tested and the regulator quadrant marked with 10 equal divisions. Finally, a new drawbar pin without any clearances was produced for coupling the locomotive to the testing station dynamometer.

The engine and its train were worked to Harwich and on Wednesday 5 December 1934 the consignment was loaded on to the train ferry before departing for Calais at 8.30pm. The following morning the ferry docked at Calais; however, the locomotive and its train were not disembarked until the afternoon due to customs formalities. Once unloaded, the engine had its fire lit and was taken to Calais Locomotive Depot under its own power by its LNER crew. The crew selected to travel with the locomotive was Driver G. Trower and Fireman W. Gant of Doncaster. Driver Trower had started work on the railway in 1893, passing as a driver in 1911 and was a regular driver on Royal Train duties. Another fireman, J. Bradley, also travelled over from Doncaster to assist for a short period.

Gresley attended on several occasions but seems to have left O. V. S Bulleid to take charge and organise the work required on the locomotive whilst Gresley remained in his office at King's Cross. Bulleid had been involved in the design work on the locomotive and, it seems, was instrumental in the adoption of the Lentz poppet valves and experimental items of equipment fitted to the locomotive. The team was also supplemented by Teddy Windle, Chief Draughtsman, J. Boulby, Chargeman Erector, and his assistant Mr Horsfull, all from the Doncaster Works.

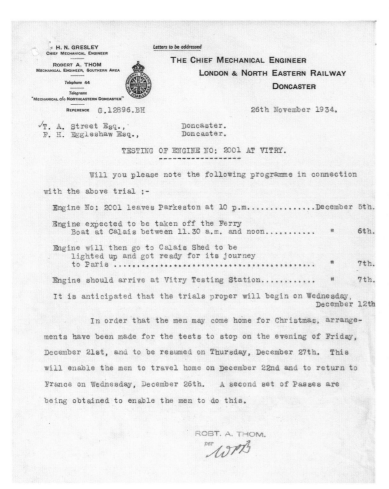

LEFT Letter from R. A. Thom with *Cock o' the North's* timetable in France. *NRM/SSP*

ABOVE Interior view of the Vitry testing station. *P2SLC Collection*

BELOW Contemporary colour print of the testing of the 'P2' at Vitry. *Mandy Grant Collection*

Leaving Calais Maritime the next day at just after 7.30am the engine proceeded along the French main lines via Amiens, Montdidier, Le Bourget, Villeneuve-Saint-Georges, Juvisy and Ivry before arriving at Vitry around 6.30pm. Throughout, the engine was worked by its Doncaster crew with a French conductor/driver and Inspector riding on the footplate. During its journey the locomotive was equipped with a large French-pattern headlamp.

Upon arrival the engine was taken to the Ouest locomotive depot before being taken to the test plant the following morning so that the rollers could be set for it. That evening a trial run of the locomotive was made for the first time under its own power.

At the time the testing station at Vitry was the most sophisticated in the world. The facility could handle the largest of locomotives. The building housed eight sets of adjustable rimless rollers on which a locomotive, minus its tender, could be placed and run at speed. The rollers were each coupled to a water brake controlled by a governor built by Heenan & Froude in Worcestershire, England, which allowed a

TOP *Cock o' the North* and its train of bogie coal wagons and brake van at Amiens station on its way to Vitry.
P2SLC Collection

ABOVE *Cock o' the North* undergoes testing.
P2SLC Collection

predetermined load to be placed upon the locomotive as it worked and the speed to be set. Should the locomotive start to accelerate, the pressure applied by the braking system on the rollers increased, slowing the locomotive down. This system proved very stable, keeping the speed within 1% either side of the desired limit.

The drawbar of the locomotive was also coupled to a hydraulic dynamometer to allow the drawbar horsepower to be recorded. Coal and water could also be measured scientifically and connections for pyrometers and other sensors were also provided. Finally, a 'stroborama' was provided for

the stroboscopic examination of the motion whilst it was moving at high speed. The facility was also equipped with a laboratory for fuel analysis and determination of calorific values of coal plus calibrating the gauges and equipment used.

The main control room was equipped with a dynametric recording table overlooking the open cab of locomotives on test from a raised view. A total of 90 sets of wires were installed for relaying signals from the testing equipment to the control room. The recording table was fitted with six main pens to record, time, distance travelled, speed, drawbar power, total effective work at the drawbar and the drawbar horsepower. These pens recorded their information on a sheet of moving paper controlled by the rollers under the locomotive. Scientific analysis of these factors, combined with measurements of coal and water, allowed for reliable readings of efficiency, power and many other factors to be measured under scientific conditions and for direct comparisons to be made between locomotives.

The first day of operation was handed over to publicity, with several journalists present for both the English and French newspapers and newsreel. Bulleid gave short interviews about the locomotive and its testing in both English and French as required.

Almost as soon as runs on the test bed started the engine started to suffer from problems. The

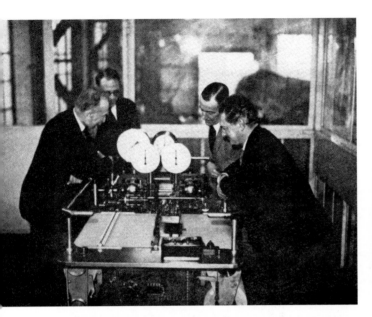

driving wheel axleboxes ran hot and showed signs of melting white metal on the bearings, a coupling rod bush ran hot and an uneven exhaust beat was heard. The coupling rod bush was quickly replaced with a spare and caused no further problems. However, the uneven exhaust beat was not easy to diagnose. Representatives from the Dabeg Company looked at the locomotive and suggested modifications but could not solve the problem. It was later suggested that the variation in clearance volumes in the cylinders could be causing it. On its return to the UK some work on these were carried out but the engine never gained a perfectly even exhaust.

The biggest headache for the engineers, however, was the axleboxes. On several occasions the wheels were dropped, the axleboxes inspected, white metal replaced and both the spare axleboxes fitted in place of ones that had overheated. However, the problem persisted and a theory began to develop that the lack of vibration on the test plant was, somewhat bizarrely, causing the oil film to rupture and localised heating to occur. On 21 December the final run was made and the men came home the following day to England to spend Christmas with their families before returning to France on New Year's Eve. In its three weeks in France the engine had been unable to undertake any serious testing.

With the new year came preparations for further attempts at testing. The opportunity was also taken to remove the back plate of the ashpan, at Bulleid's request, to see if the vast amounts of black smoke that the engine had been known to produce could be eased. Unfortunately, this modification made little difference and Bulleid

later joked that when he was travelling to the testing plant by motorcar he could tell if the engine was already in steam due to the black smoke being emitted from the building's extractors. No 2001 was again placed on the test plant after the rollers had been reset owing to the testing of a French 'Est' locomotive testing during the Christmas period. Great care was taken to ensure the rollers were perfectly aligned to ensure that the wheels did not move on the rollers which was another theory given for the axlebox overheating. However, the engine ran hot again and the Paris office of the Wakefield Oil Company was summoned to check over the engine's lubrication system. No faults were found but a new oil was specified for the tests, this making no difference with the locomotive, which again overheated.

On 26 January 1935 the engine was given a short run on the main line at 25mph to help bed in the bearings that had once again been white metalled. No signs of overheating were found and the engine returned to the test bed and not long afterwards the overheating of bearings started again. As the Paris workshops had limited lifting facilities a decision was made to send the engine along the French main line to Tours where the engine could be lifted and fully examined. This was arranged for 31 January. However, on arrival at Tours the bearings on the engine were found to be completely cold and the French engineer who examined it recommended that the engine did not need lifting. After conferring with the English engineers at Vitry it was decided not to lift the engine and also to arrange two trips to Orléans, a distance of

ABOVE LEFT Bulleid and a test engineer study the readouts from the dynamometer table. *P2SLC Collection*

ABOVE RIGHT Driver Trower and Fireman Gant at work with the engine on test. *P2SLC Collection*

72 miles in each direction, for the following day. These journeys were carried out non-stop at an average speed of 60mph over the two trips, with a top speed of 82.8mph recorded on the footplate. During the trips there were no signs of the bearings overheating.

With the engine now seemingly settled down a new shortened set of tests were proposed to and agreed by Gresley. Five tests would be carried out, four being consumption tests at 90km/h with drawbar horsepower between 750 and 2,250 horsepower and a maximum power test at 90km/h with full regulator and 35% cut-off. However, before the engine returned to Vitry, it was arranged for the locomotive to work three test trains with a French dynamometer car and three out-of-steam four-cylinder compound engines to provide resistance by way of counter-pressure testing. During these tests the maximum power was recorded as 1,910 horsepower at an average of 80.7km/h. During these tests the opportunity was given to the French crews to operate the locomotive. The fireman found the boiler pressure hard to maintain during the tests, with one driver commenting that the firehole door was not large enough and that the standard issue LNER shovel provided was half the size of a French shovel, requiring undue effort from the fireman, although he did concede that overall he found the locomotive 'magnificent'.

The engine was returned to Vitry and placed on the test plant and the testing commenced. The engine performed better at first, although it was found that maintaining the boiler pressure for increased periods of time was troublesome and some of the axleboxes started to get a little warm. By good fortune Bulleid was standing at the side of the engine as it was undergoing its testing when he noticed the right-hand-side leading driving wheel was showing 'the familiar signs of incipient heating'. He immediately stopped the tests and examined the bearings and axleboxes and found them to be cold, but rather than continuing the test he withdrew the locomotive for examination, finding that a piece of white metal about the size of a five shilling piece had been torn off the face in line with the centre of the frames. Examination of the other axleboxes showed similar failures occurring. He later said that 'for the first time we had clear evidence that the failure was due to the rupture of the oil film and all theories could be discarded. In view of this I decided to return the engine to England.' Interestingly, it was later discovered that French engines suffered the same faults when tested for long periods on the Vitry plant, the lack of vibration by the ultra modern scientific facility causing the previously unseen phenomenon.

With the locomotive's testing completed, arrangements were put in place for the locomotive

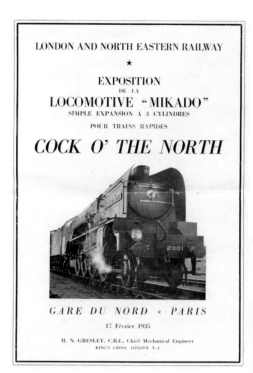

LONDON AND NORTH EASTERN RAILWAY

★

EXPOSITION
DE LA
LOCOMOTIVE "MIKADO"
SIMPLE EXPANSION A 3 CYLINDRES

POUR TRAINS RAPIDES

COCK O' THE NORTH

GARE DU NORD ★ PARIS

17 Février 1935

H. N. GRESLEY, C.B.E., Chief Mechanical Engineer
KING'S CROSS, LONDON N.1.

to be exhibited at Paris Gare du Nord station. The engine left Vitry at 10.30am on 14 February with its train of British rolling stock and proceeded to the Nord locomotive shops at La Chapelle. Whilst on route at Villeneuve St Georges, two of the LNER coal wagons were removed from the train. Their contents, approximately 80 tons of Yorkshire coal, were then taken on by the P.L.M. Railway who wished to carry out trials with it on its own locomotives. The train then continued via Le Borget, arriving at 4.30pm. The following two days were spent cleaning and preparing the locomotive, including the interior of the smokebox and the locomotive cab, for exhibition,.

On Sunday 17 the engine was placed on display in Platform 1 of Paris Gare du Nord

station, accompanied by Mr Besnerais' (the deputy chief operating officer of the Chemin de fur du Nord) personal saloon coach, and a Nord Super Pacific, No 1268. The exhibition was open to the public from 11.30am until 7pm and it is reported that several thousand people visited, the event having been advertised in the local newspapers.

During the exhibition one of the Maybach diesel-electric streamlined railcars arrived in Platform 2 and took part in the exhibition and seemingly impressed the English crew and engineers present. At the end of the exhibition the locomotive was returned to La Chapelle.

On the following Wednesday the engine was prepared for its final working over French metals, returning to Calais via Montdidier, Amiens and Étaples. The engine and train of now empty coal wagons, stores van and brakevan were worked by its English crew accompanied by a French pilot driver and Inspector riding on the locomotive, with the journey taking a little over eight hours. The following day was spent completing Customs formalities and loading the engine and stock on the train ferry before the ferry left for Harwich in the evening. With the locomotive back on English soil, a relieving crew worked the engine back to Doncaster whilst the men that had worked the engine in France were allowed to return home as passengers.

TOP LEFT Detail of the water-brake rollers. *P2SLC Collection*

TOP RIGHT Cover from the French leaflet produced while the engine was on display in Paris *P2SLC Collection*

CENTRE LEFT With No 2001 on test a test engineer studies the readings from the control room. *P2SLC Collection*

ABOVE *Cock o' the North*, complete with French locomotive headlamps, is prepared for its journey from Vitry back to Calais. *P2SLC Collection*

LEFT No 2001 on show in company with a directors' saloon and a Nord Super-Pacific at Paris Gare du Nord on 19 February 1935. *P2SLC Collection*

CHAPTER 6

THE STREAMLINED MIKADOS

As previously described, *Cock o' the North* travelled to France for testing on the Vitry-sur-Seine testing station. After the locomotive returned to the UK, the railway community expected it to return quickly to Scotland. However, it spent some considerable time working from London and Doncaster before finally being returned to Haymarket in June 1935.

No 2002 was transferred to Scotland from Doncaster on 8 June 1935 and spent the first 13 days at Edinburgh Haymarket before being transferred to Dundee Tay Bridge shed on 22 June. *Earl Marischal* was entrusted to the capable hands of two regular crews, Driver G. Arbuthnott and Driver T. Campbell.

During the summer of 1935, the renowned railway author O. S. Nock travelled to Scotland with the sole intention of travelling on the footplate of the two new 'P2' locomotives and wrote about his experiences and impressions of the engines.

His first account involved a morning train from Aberdeen to Dundee on Saturday 3 August 1935. Leaving Aberdeen at 10.20am with its 515-ton train, *Earl Marischal* was immediately opened up to full regulator by Driver Arbuthnot and after the first mile the cut-off was shortened to 25%. The engine accelerated into the hefty climb towards Girdle Ness Lighthouse before the speed fell to 35.5mph on the steepest part of the ascent of 1 in 102 past Cove Bay station, having taken just 13 minutes from Dundee. This time was consistent with other journeys over the same stretch hauled by Caledonian 4-4-0s and North British Atlantics, although with substantially lighter loads of 250 and 300 tons respectively. Continuing to Stonehaven, the author next wrote about the ease with which the locomotive restarted its train from Stonehaven and climbed Dunnottar bank. Again with full regulator and 32% cut-off, the engine attacked the 1 in 90 gradient, accelerating to 32.5mph before the easing of the gradient at Dunnottar signal box, where the slight easing of the gradient allowed the cut-off to be adjusted to 25%, at which point the engine continued to climb the bank at ease. The train carried on to Arbroath where the author alighted, opting to return to Aberdeen for a break before a second evening run on No 2002.

On the same day, Nock made the same journey on *Earl Marischal* on the 7.35pm Aberdeen to Edinburgh, travelling with No 2002 this time throughout to Dundee with Driver Campbell. The run proved nothing spectacular with steady gentle running allowing a relaxed and on-time arrival at Dundee. On both trips Nock noted that the engine rode well, stating that 'another impression of this grand engine was of the buoyant and luxurious way in which the curves were taken. We had plenty of brisk running downhill at 65 to 70mph and the engine rode superbly on curves and straights alike.' He also noted how the locomotive was the master of the work and handled it with relative quiet and ease compared with the thunderous cacophony of the smaller locomotives he was more acquainted with. The only difference noted by the author between the two trips was the coal consumption. On the second trip the engine was driven with only a partially opened regulator and longer cut-offs and it was noted that the boiler pressure fluctuated to a greater degree whilst running on the road than on the morning trip. This method was not

normally recognised as the correct way of driving Gresley's express locomotives and as such would possibly have led to the heavier coal consumption as noted by Nock.

On arrival at Dundee Nock joined the 40 or so people who had gathered to witness the changing of locomotives prior to the train continuing on the Up 'Aberdonian', continuing to Edinburgh. The 7.35pm train from Aberdeen was the only occasion on the regular daily roster during this period when the two 'P2' class locomotives would be seen together, one relieving the other for the train to continue. Nock took the opportunity to excuse himself from the footplate of *Earl Marischal* before boarding the footplate of *Cock o' the North* to complete the trip to Edinburgh with Driver Sheddon and Fireman Hardisty. Leaving Dundee, the locomotive immediately set to work against the steep gradient and Driver Sheddon started to notch up the engine, fixing the gear at 25% as it passed through Dundee Esplanade. The engine continued to climb up onto the Tay Bridge, working at full regulator, before reaching the

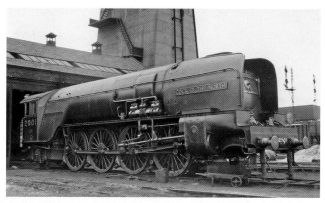

level section half way over the Tay, where the engine was again notched up to 18% and the speed was allowed to increase to 60mph. Passing St Fort the regulator was completely shut and its free-running characteristics meant that a slight touch of the brakes was required to ease the speed to 55mph for Leuchars Junction. The engine was then eased into the incline leading to Ladybank Junction before a touch of the brakes for the restriction through the station. After the station, half a mile of level running gave a brief respite and a chance to increase speed to 60mph before the start of Falkland Road bank, with 3.5 miles of 1 in 100 rising gradient. To the surprise of Nock, the locomotive was continuously worked in 18% gear with the 530-ton train climbing the bank in remarkable style, passing the summit near Lochmuir at 26mph. The train continued to Thornton, where a 10mph permanent way slack caused the train to be slowed through the junction before the train was accelerated uphill to Dysart. On the downhill section running towards Kirkcaldy the speed increased to 55mph before steam was shut off completely. However, with the free running of the engine, attributed to the decreased resistance of the poppet valves, the train continued to accelerate passing Kirkcaldy at 65mph before running several further miles on the level at 60mph with no steam being admitted to the cylinders. The brakes were applied again to bring the train's speed down to 25mph at both Kinghorn tunnel and Burntisland. The regulator was once again opened wide for the climb to Dalgetty and on the steepening gradients the cut-off was lengthened to 25% before the summit was reached at 31mph. The line once again descended towards Inverkeithing and steam was again shut off in anticipation of the 25mph slack around Inverkeithing curve. Immediately following this restriction came the most ferocious gradient on the route, the 1 in 70

climb for two miles up to the Forth Bridge. On the downhill stretch the reverser had been set once again to 18% but as the train passed Inverkeithing this was lengthened to 25% for the start of the climb and, with 210psi in the boiler and an almost fully open regulator, the engine

TOP LEFT *Cock o' the North* in rather dirty condition works an express service away from Edinburgh. *Transport Treasury*

TOP RIGHT *Cock o' the North* receives attention to its swing link pony truck at Haymarket depot. *P2SLC Collection*

ABOVE Leaving Aberdeen, No 2001 hauls a heavy express bound for Edinburgh. *Transport Treasury*

LEFT No 2001 being prepared ready for its next duty at Edinburgh Haymarket depot. *P2SLC Collection*

held a steady 25mph for the first half of the climb. Just as the train approached North Queensferry tunnel the driver once again lengthened the cut-off to the next cam set at 35%. With this the engine erupted and started to work really hard, sending little white slabs of fire from the chimney into the tunnel. The train emerged from the tunnel at 19mph and headed out over the water on the Forth Bridge. Speed started to rise but the driver held it back in anticipation of the junction at Dalmeny before allowing the engine to run towards Turnhouse, reaching 68mph and sustaining high speeds on the run into the outskirts of Edinburgh. Haymarket station was passed before the train

entered into the tunnels heading towards the famous castle and emerging into the deep cutting at Princes Street Gardens before a careful approach through the station throat. Arrival at Edinburgh Waverley was within 3 seconds of scheduled time. Nock was impressed by both locomotives and their capabilities and although he noted that both were masters of their work he thought *Cock o' the North* was heavier on coal than its piston valve relative. As such it seems No 2002 became his preferred locomotive, writing several years later that his lasting impression was 'of the superb work of *Earl Marischal*, in the hands of Driver Arbuthnot and Fireman Coming. It is not too much to say that she was the most puissant British locomotive I have ever set foot upon, even including some of the Stanier 'Pacifics'.'

However the first P2s did not have an unblemished record during their early days in Scotland. On Saturday 28 September No 2002 was working the 10.20am train from Aberdeen to Edinburgh as far as Dundee when it failed with a hot axlebox at Montrose. The locomotive was removed from the 510-ton train and replaced by a 'J36' class locomotive, No 9776, which was assisted at Arbroath to Dundee by a 'G9' class 0-4-4 tank. Remarkably, it was reported that the train only lost 22 minutes in running between Montrose and Dundee.

With the successful entry into service of the first two members of the class, the LNER proceeded with the construction of a further four locomotives. These engines had originally been authorised at the same time as *Earl Marischal* but were then held back pending the

ABOVE LEFT No 2003 under construction. *P2SLC Collection*

ABOVE RIGHT No 2005 in the workshops at Doncaster shortly after being wheeled for the first time. *P2SLC Collection*

LEFT Works photograph of a freshly completed *Lord President*. *NRM/SSPL*

construction and trials of No 2002. This last batch of 'P2s' was broadly similar to No 2002 although each had subtle differences. However, there was one major difference between the new locomotives and *Earl Marischal*, this being the inclusion of the fully streamlined front end as used on the 'A4' class engines to help with the smoke clearance problems suffered by No 2002 before the addition of the extra smoke deflectors.

During the mid 1930s high-speed rail travel was becoming increasingly glamorous. The 'A4' class was Gresley's answer to the fast inter-city travel introduced in Germany using new diesel railcars. The LNER was interested in such a scheme and although the Chief Engineer travelled on the new railcars he was adamant that the same style of working could be achieved with new steam locomotives. This was reaffirmed

ABOVE LEFT The 'A4'-styled front end of No 2003. *NRM/SSPL*

ABOVE RIGHT *Lord President* on display at Doncaster Works on 20 June 1936.

Ian Allan Library

when the manufacturers could not provide Gresley with a railcar solution to meet the timings required on the new streamlined express. With the construction of *Cock o' the North* nearing completion, the attention of its designer turned to the new high-speed class. Various elements of the 'P2' design, including the streamlined passageways and streamlined cab, were incorporated into the new class. The front end, however, was a completely new design, modelled on the Bugatti-designed petrol railcar operating in France. Drawings were prepared based on this design showing a main radius of 12ft for the front curve instead of the 14ft of the railcars. This detail went unnoticed by Gresley and the drawing office staff until it was too late,

the mistake being incorporated into the 'A4s' and later the 'P2', rebuilt 'W1' and 'B17/5' classes rather than being corrected. Prior to construction, wind tunnel testing was once again carried out by Professor Dalby to ensure the front end would clear smoke and steam satisfactorily. The first locomotive, *Silver Link* was completed in September 1935 and entered service on the new 'Silver Jubilee' service between London and Newcastle. Construction of the 'A4s' continued, with the class numbering a total of 35 including *Mallard* which, on 3 July 1938, broke the world record for the fastest steam locomotive ever recorded with a speed of 126mph.

Gresley incorporated the successful front end design on all of the remaining 'P2' locomotives,

solving the smoke drifting issues. It was also planned to fit the engines with the streamlined aerofoil side skirts fitted to the 'A4s' but these were dropped in favour of a straight running plate. Construction of the new engines began in early 1936 with the first locomotive, No 2003 *Lord President*, being completed on 13 June 1936 as Doncaster works number 1836. Other than the streamlined front end, the engine was the same as No 2002 and became recognised as the standard model of streamlined 'P2'. From new, the engine was allocated to Edinburgh Haymarket depot but was soon sent to Dundee Tay Bridge three months later, where it was used until it was once again transferred to Haymarket in October 1942.

The next engine, No 2004 *Mons Meg*, was completed the following month, leaving Doncaster with the allocated works number of 1839. The locomotive was identical to its sister engine No 2003 except for one subtle difference. In an attempt to reduce the ferocious blast from the locomotive's exhaust and the detrimental effect of pulling the fire too hard that resulted, a by-pass valve was fitted to divert part of the exhaust steam away from the blastpipe. Originally a butterfly valve was fitted and this was opened by pulling a mechanical linkage that ran along the left-hand side of the locomotive behind the vacuum ejector pipe. However, oil often carbonised in the valve and it would get stuck open or closed, causing the locomotive to be failed. The draughtsman who designed the valve, L. Parker, was sent from Doncaster to unstick and sort the valve out at Thornton, eventually coming up with a new design. In July 1937 it was changed to a plug-type valve, pulled to open and pushed to shut, again using a mechanical linkage. However, it was noted that its use was ignored by drivers as it could make the locomotive steam badly on uphill stretches of line. Parker was once again sent north and after

riding on the locomotive found the mechanical linkages seized due to lack of use. A redesign was required and in June 1939 it was replaced by an automatic valve working off a linkage on the reverser which opened the valve when cut-off was 38% or longer in forward gear. Problems with carbonisation still occurred, requiring frequent dismantling and cleaning during maintenance and washout periods. More proposals were put forward during 1940 including an automatic flap-valve and a steam

ABOVE CENTRE No 2003 at Newark with a short train during running-in trials in June 1936. *Rail Archive Stephenson*

ABOVE *Lord President* on shed at Dundee Tay Bridge. *P2SLC Collection*

operated valve but neither option was ever taken past the design stage. During its life as a 2-8-2, the engine was continuously based at Haymarket shed, only leaving for maintenance work at Cowlairs in Glasgow or Doncaster.

The penultimate member of the 'P2' class entered traffic on 8 August 1936. No 2005 *Thane of Fife* emerged from Doncaster gaining the works number 1840 and equipped with boiler 8799. After running in, the locomotive was sent to Scotland and allocated to Dundee Tay Bridge shed, where it remained for its entire life as a 'P2'. *Thane of Fife* was yet another variation on the 'P2' theme, being almost identical to No 2003 *Lord President* except that it was equipped with a single chimney. Originally Gresley had looked at the possibility of fitting No 2002 with a single chimney but declined this in favour of the double

chimney so that the engine could be used as a direct comparison with No 2001.

No 2005 would be the only 'P2' fitted with a single chimney, underneath which was a 6in blastpipe orifice. Some of the 'A4' class Pacific's were fitted with single chimneys equipped with jumper-top blast pipes These devices allowed the strong blast of the locomotive exhaust to lift the outer casing of the jumper top which then increased the size of the blastpipe orifice and improved the locomotive's performance. A decision was made to fit this device to No 2005 in December 1938, with actual fitment taking place during a works visit in April 1939. With the jumper-top fitted and in operation the blastpipe orifice on *Thane of Fife* could be increased from 6 inches to 6¾ inches. No 2005, however, was always seen as the black sheep of the 'P2' class, with footplate crews often citing the single chimney as a hindrance compared to the other engines. However, the engine kept the single chimney.

The final member of the 'P2' class entered traffic on 5 September 1936. No 2006 was given the name *Wolf of Badenoch* and the works number 1842. Like the other engines in the last batch of 'P2s', the locomotive featured a streamlined front end, Walschaerts valve gear and piston valves. Although it was planned to fit the engine with an identical design of boiler to the other engines, the decision was made to fit the engine with a new diagram 108 pattern boiler. This boiler was a modified form of the 'A4' boiler (diagram 107) and featured a larger combustion chamber to help complete total combustion and required the two tube plates to be placed closer together. The locomotive's originally ordered boiler was kept as a spare, being utilised on No 2002 when the latter's own

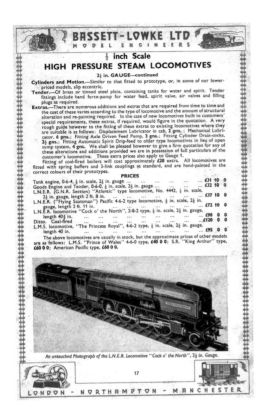

boiler was due for repairs. The inclusion of a larger combustion chamber was suggest by Bulleid, who calculated that moving the tubeplates 1ft closer together, and correspondingly making the combustion chamber 1ft longer would improve combustion. A larger volume of air space in the fire grate was incorporated in the new design, this later being utilised on the entire class. The enlarged firebox meant that three extra rows of roof stays were fitted along with five inspection doors on each side of the boiler. Overall, the total heating surface of the boiler was 3,346.5sq ft, comprising an increased firebox heating surface of 252.5sq.ft, a reduction in the heating surface of the tubes to 1,281.4sq ft and the flues to 1,063.7sq ft, with a corresponding reduction in the superheater heating surface to 748.9sq ft. This boiler later became the prototype for the 118a boiler design which was used on Thompson's and Peppercorn's 'A1' class locomotives.

From new the streamlined engines were painted in a similar fashion to the 'A4s', with the wedge-shaped front painted black and separated from the main engine colour with a parabolic curve.

FAR LEFT Advert from the model engineering firm of Bassett-Lowke featuring the 'P2' as its flagship live steam working model. *P2SLC Collection*

ABOVE Nos 2003 and 2006 are prepared for their respective trains at Aberdeen Ferryhill. *William Pounder (Maurice Burns Archive)*

BELOW *Thane of Fife* ready for the off at Dundee Tay Bridge depot. *P2SLC Collection*

However, unlike the 'A4s', where the standard colour was Garter Blue, the 'P2s' continued with the more traditional Apple Green for the body work. The new 'P2s' were also given Streamlined Non-Corridor tenders similar to a number of 'A4' and 'A3' Pacifics. Like the engine parts, these tenders were ordered as Order Number 62 on 7 November 1933, with construction deferred until the testing of No 2002 was completed. The tenders shared the identical capacity of coal and water to their earlier siblings but were visually different. The beading around the edges was omitted whilst the front edges of the tender were also kept straight to match the profile of the cabs of Nos 2003-6, which themselves had straight edges rather than the curved variety of the earlier LNER Pacifics. The tablet exchanger equipment was fitted and operated through an elliptical hole cut in the cab end of the left-hand tender side sheet. Extra valancing was provided on the tender top although this was altered in later life. The tenders ran on steel disc centred wheels as per LNER standard practice. Interestingly these four tenders stayed with the class their entire lives, including the later rebuilding by Thompson, the only swap being between No 2005 and No 2006 in 1945.

In keeping with *Cock o' the North*, the new 'P2s' were also given names featured in Scottish folklore. In late 1934 Gresley and the LNER Advertising Department gave the opportunity to Scottish Boy Scouts to choose names for the new locomotives in a competition, with the winners receiving a prize. The January 1935 edition of the *Railway Magazine* reported:

> 'LNER Engine Name Competition – Boy Scouts were asked to suggest names for the new 2-8-2 engines which the L.N.E.R. intend building for their Scottish lines. Over

two thousand entries were received and although the railway company does not bind itself to use the names submitted, there is the probability some may be finally chosen for the new engines. The prize-winners are to be given a free trip to the Doncaster Works, as well as a guinea pocket money. They are as follows: H. R. Watson, who suggested the name Earl Marischal, which has been chosen for engine No 2002; J. N. Wheatley, Gordon of Fochabers; J. M. Laing, Maid of Glamis; R. Edminson, Mons Meg; and D. E. Townley, Thane of Fife.'

Out of the remaining winning names *Mons Meg* and *Thane of Fife* were both chosen to be carried on the new engines. *Mons Meg* was named after the much celebrated 15-century cannon that stands high above Waverley station on the ramparts of Edinburgh Castle and was given to No 2004 whilst No 2005 received *Thane of Fife*, the ancient name given to the Earl of Fife (whose territory the Aberdeen line passes through). The latter name was not new to the LNER, having been carried by a North British Atlantic withdrawn in January 1935. The other new engines were given the names *Lord President*, the title given to the head of the Court of Session that sat in Edinburgh, the Scottish equivalent to the Lord Chief Justice, which was given to No 2003, whilst No 2006 received *Wolf of Badenoch*, the name given to Alexander Stewart, the Earl of Buchan (1343-1405), the fourth son of King Robert II of Scotland. He had earned the nickname because of his ruthless treatment of his enemies and the burning down of Elgin Cathedral in 1390.

With the streamlined engines now in service, attention once again turned to the original pair of locomotives to bring their aesthetics into line

LEFT *Cock o' the North*, rebuilt as a streamliner, is turned on the turntable ready for its next working at Haymarket.
P2SLC Collection

with their more modern sisters. During its first heavy repair at Doncaster Works in October 1936, *Earl Marischal* had its front end rebuilt to conform to the streamlined engines. Likewise, when *Cock o' the North* received its first heavy repair in September 1937, the opportunity was taken to rebuild the engine in line with the other members of the class. This work, however, was more complicated, involving the removal of the poppet valves and associated gear and the casting of a new cylinder block incorporating piston valves operated by Walschaerts valve gear along with removal of the ACFI feedwater heater and its replacement with a traditional exhaust steam injector. Emerging fully streamlined from Doncaster Works in April 1938, No 2001 completed the class of six streamlined 2-8-2s.

Although it had been envisaged that the engines would haul trains throughout the entire length of the Edinburgh to Aberdeen route, the powers that be soon decided against this. No

official reason was ever given but several contemporary writers suggest that it was due to the locomotives' hunger for coal, with the risk of supplies running low on the road and the physical effort needed by the firemen to work the engines. As a result the diagrams for the 'P2s' were amended, with one engine working the trains from Edinburgh to Dundee and another taking the train forward from Dundee to Aberdeen. The return workings would be handled in the same manner, with one engine working the Northern section and the other the Southern section. This manner of working, however, proved to be less than economic, with the engines spending prolonged periods of time on shed waiting for their next working, burning large amounts of coal on their 50sq ft grate whilst carrying out no useful revenue earning work, a fact overlooked by the locomotives' critics who thought that the excessive coal was burnt during running. Bulleid, however, was aware of this fact

ABOVE No 2002 heads a heavy fitted fast fish and milk service away from Aberdeen.
P2SLC Collection

from the outset and whilst discussing *Cock o' the North* at a meeting of the Institute of Locomotive Engineers in 1947 said:

'In service, however, it was an extravagant engine as it was not properly used: instead of working trains well within its capacity over long runs, it was employed on a service such as Edinburgh to Dundee on trains much under its capacity; it stood for a long time at Dundee, went to Aberdeen and hung about there, and did a very poor mileage per day, with the result that it showed a heavy coal consumption, most of the coal being burnt through misuse rather than in working trains.'

Bulleid always deemed the engines to be successful handling the trains they were designed to haul with ease.

The locomotives, however, were needed to haul all the heavy principal trains over the Aberdeen line and the diagrams were designed so that an engine would be available for these. The LNER Operating Department and Gresley were both in agreement that the best performances from the Mikados would be achieved if the engines each received regular crews. This was particularly the case with the

first two engines in their original condition as the differences in driving technique were quite substantial. Each engine would receive two crews who would work the various turns on a rota. Haymarket depot allocated drivers A. Douglas and A. Shedden and firemen W. Graham and J. Cunningham to *Cock o' the North* whilst Dundee Tay Bridge rostered drivers G. Arbuthnott and T. Campbell and firemen C. Winter and E. Stephens to *Earl Marischal*. The practice of pairing set crews and locomotives was not new on the LNER as the introduction of new classes, experimental locomotives and special workings all warranted crews to be assigned to set work. This could also have been another reason for the locomotives' split working along the route. It seems that Haymarket men did not work trains north of Dundee, most of their focus being south from Edinburgh. Accordingly, the nickname given to the men who did work trains north was the 'Dundees', giving evidence to the fact that they worked only as far as that location. This practice stemmed back to North British Railway Company days when the tradition was to exchange crews at Dundee. This lack of route knowledge for the Haymarket men would necessitate the engine being taken over by another crew to continue the train forwards and it seems that the LNER was reluctant for too

ABOVE *Thane of Fife* at work on a fast freight.
P2SLC Collection

many people to be involved with the new engines, resulting in the decision to swap the engines over at Dundee.

With only two Mikados available the diagramming involved both engines making two round trips over their respective sections of the railway. After the introduction of the four streamlined examples in 1936 the diagramming became a little easier with a greater selection of services and expresses being covered by the engines. This certainly helped the situation at the depots and all but eliminated the pilot working needed before the introduction of the 'P2s'. Aberdeen Ferryhill shed also gained a pair of 'P2' engines but interestingly they did not get their own crews. Instead, the engines were used by any crews in the No 1 Link on express passenger duties or by crews in the No 2 link on fast fish and meat trains. Other than during a short period following the introduction of the streamlined locomotives, split working continued with engines taking over from each other at Dundee. During the aforementioned period of through running it was possible to see all six members of the class at Edinburgh Waverley during the day, which is believed to

have been the only time this was possible. With the split running, Haymarket engines worked north to Dundee, and Ferryhill engines worked south to the same location, whilst the Dundee engines worked in both directions. Obviously there were occasions where engines would work off their normal patch due to faults or failures on other engines or between movements to or from depots for maintenance. Interestingly there were some diagrams where the same locomotive would work a train over the entire length of the line with the crews still changing as per the normal practice. One such diagram appeared in 1937 with two Dundee crews working one engine over the entire line. The engine was worked from Dundee to Edinburgh on an unrecorded train before working the 2pm Edinburgh to Aberdeen express, complete with restaurant cars. This train was a continuation of the 4.45am King's Cross to Edinburgh service. The engine worked to Dundee where the crews swapped at 3.29pm before continuing to Aberdeen arriving at 5.49pm. Just under two hours were then allowed for the engine to be serviced at Ferryhill depot before the engine worked the Up 'Aberdonian', usually forming a load of over 500 tons back to

RIGHT *Lord President* receives attention inside Doncaster Works in company with 'A3' *Grand Parade* (under construction) on 3 April 1938.

Rail Archive Stephenson

Dundee at 7.35pm. The engine would then be swapped for a Haymarket-allocated 'P2' for its onward journey to Edinburgh. It was on this sort of diagram that the engines came into their own hauling the heavy trains with ease and punctuality. Photographic evidence also proves that through working was used on a semi regular basis, with images of both Haymarket and Aberdeen-allocated engines being used on the 'wrong' side of Dundee. Taking the split crewing arrangements into account, it is worth noting that the Dundee men had the closest association with the class, working all the fleet in both directions along the Aberdeen line due to their location and route knowledge.

The 'P2s', however, started to gain a reputation for derailments and track spreading, this being one of the most common stories retold by commentators and enthusiasts about the class today. These faults were alleged by some writers and commentators several years after the original engines were rebuilt or indeed scrapped, stemming from the idea that the long fixed wheelbase of the locomotives caused them to derail. Looking at contemporary sources there is no evidence that the locomotives caused damage to the track. It is also worth considering that the engines ran daily over sections of line owned by the London, Midland & Scottish Railway, who would have taken issue with or possibly banned the locomotives from operating had there been such regular occurrences as described by some authors.

Likewise, it is difficult to find any evidence that the engines frequently derailed. The company was aware that the engine's wheelbase may cause problems in locomotive depots where the track condition would often be less than satisfactory, resulting in the Operating Department publishing a notice that the engines were to be operated with care within these areas. Nothing can be found to prove that the engines ever came to grief on the main line although there is evidence of No 2002 becoming derailed at King's Cross depot. On 29 December 1934 *Earl Marischal*'s pony wheels derailed whilst negotiating the track in the locomotive depot. The engine was soon re-railed and the engine examined at the shed, with no obvious defects being found, whilst the Civil Engineers also examined the track, again finding no faults. The decision was made however to send the engine back to the plant for a thorough examination and on 2 January the engine worked the 8.15am vacuum-braked goods train from London to Doncaster before entering the works the following day. As at Top Shed, no immediate defects could be found so the decision was made to take the engine round to the iron foundry. Outside the old iron foundry at Doncaster Works the track work featured a particularly sharp curve on which the engineers used to test all large locomotives before they were allowed to enter service. All of the Mikados, including No 2002; along with the Pacifics, had been tested around this curve under strict conditions before

LEFT Photo of the broken crank axle of No 2005 that occurred on 19 July 1939. The axle was 2 years and 11 months old and had covered only 133,000 miles.
P2SLC Collection

entering service. *Earl Marischal* had already passed this test but the decision was made to repeat the experiment and a shunting locomotive was found and attached to the tender, ready to push the engine around the curve under observation of the Works staff. The engine traversed the corner satisfactorily but a problem occurred when the shunting engine derailed on the same curve behind the engine. Once the shunter had been re-railed the engine was returned to the workshop. During these movements one of the staff noticed a slightly irregular movement in the pony wheels. After examination and careful measurement it was found that the pony axle was slightly bent, requiring replacement, and the derailment was attributed to the fault. As a precaution the minimum curvature was amended from six chains to seven chains. Depot derailments were frequent during the 1930s, especially in areas where track maintenance were poor, with members of most locomotive classes coming to grief at some point during their operation

Whilst in the works the opportunity was also taken to measure the actual sideways movement of the pony truck to compare it with the calculated theoretical value. The front pony was placed on a greased plate and the truck physically moved with the movement of 3½ inches being measured. The theoretical value gave 4½ inches so the decision was made to increase the length of the swing links between their pin centres from 7in to 8in, increasing the actual movement to the planned theoretical value. This modification was also implemented on *Cock o' the North* on its return from France during a works visit in March 1935 and also incorporated from new in the streamlined 'P2' engines.

However, this modification did not solve all the problems with swing links. When the engines were in traffic the swing link pin holes quickly wore, causing the front pony to function incorrectly. This caused the engine's leading coupled wheels to guide it into the corners, causing excessive wear on the outside crankpins for the coupling rods, requiring regular attention and replacement along with cases of overheating axleboxes.

Another problem caused partially by the swing links and partially by the huge piston load of 34 tons was the overheating of the middle big end bearings. The bearing was based on a slightly enlarged 'A3' design including a larger crank pin. Calculations showed that the thrust of the piston gave over 9.5 tons of twisting force on the crank pin, a low figure when compared to the 11.2 tons of force applied to the 'A3' crank axle. A driver spotting a hot middle big end would usually fail the locomotive and refer the engine to a fitter; however spotting the fault on the road could be very difficult without the use of a pit to examine the inside gear of the engine. Unfortunately, a hot big end could lead to further problems for the engine, including scouring to the crank pins and damage to the connecting rod, piston rod, piston head and cylinder covers.

In extreme cases the stresses on the crank axle caused the crank axle itself to fail and records show this occurring on a number of occasions. The first time was on 18 July 1939 when *Thane of Fife* broke its crank axle directly next to the right-hand driving wheel, leaving Stonehaven with the 7.35am Aberdeen to King's Cross train, weighing a total of 508 tons. The engine was less than three years old at the time of the failure. The next occasion occurred on 27 May 1942 when *Mons Meg* broke its crank axle whilst starting the 2pm Edinburgh to Aberdeen express away from Kirkcaldy. The last known occasion was on 29 July 1944 when *Lord President* failed with a broken crank axle two miles south of Aberdeen whilst working the 8.50am Aberdeen to Edinburgh express. On each of these occasions the engines were running at low speed starting their trains when the forces on the crank axle would be at

their highest. Several other occasions of crank axle failure have unofficially been recorded, including on a train arriving at Edinburgh Waverley, but no official documentation about these have been found.

Maintenance facilities in Scotland were fairly limited and as such the engines were either sent to Cowlairs for the more minor repairs or back to Doncaster works for more major work. Officially the engines' minimum mileage between repairs was 70,000 miles. However, during the pre-war years the locomotives often far exceeded this, with one example, No 2006, reaching 118,930 miles from new before its first heavy general overhaul. During the Austerity years of World War 2 the mileages between major repairs fell due to the standard of care and maintenance afforded by the Scottish sheds. However, the engines' annual mileage and the mileages between heavy maintenance were on average similar to the Scottish-allocated Pacifics which, considering the sub-standard levels of maintenance they received, showed the quality of their design.

During World War 2 the railways were put under immense strain and often the most efficient rostering and locomotive allocation was not utilised. As a result the 'P2s' were used for special workings away from their usual stomping ground, for example *Mons Meg* being noted on troop trains between Perth and Newcastle. Similarly it seems that the Haymarket engines, No 2001 and No 2004, started to work occasional passenger trains to Glasgow alongside the

Pacifics. Previously, trips along the Glasgow line were only associated with positioning moves to Eastfield depot ready for maintenance at Cowlairs. Rumours of the engines' use on trains to Carlisle have persisted, although no evidence has ever come forward that they ever carried out work on the route. However during the design stage Gresley did write to the relevant locomotive superintendents to ask their opinion on injector sizes for the new locomotive, should it be used on the route. The austerity years also saw the Haymarket and Dundee engines lose their regular crews, utilising any drivers from within the link. This allowed greater flexibility of working for the Operating Department and Shed Foreman, especially if the engines were needed at short notice for special workings. With the relaxed crewing requirements it seems that through running of the locomotives between Edinburgh and Aberdeen increased. This working, however, continued to allocate two sets of crews, with the enginemen changing at Dundee Tay Bridge. Wartime conditions took their toll on the class. The conditions in Scotland were not always as good as those south of the border when it came to locomotive maintenance and contemporary evidence and photographs suggest the engines had a hard working life. However, they continued their work quietly and thoroughly throughout the first part of the war without attracting much attention from the powers that be except for the eyes of Edward Thompson, who would soon become Gresley's successor.

CHAPTER 7

THOMPSON TAKES OVER

On 5 April 1941 Gresley died whilst still in office just two months before he was due to retire. World War 2 was in its third year and austerity measures had bitten the United Kingdom hard. The halcyon years of the Gresley expresses were over and the railways were turning to wartime working requirements. Due to the sudden nature of Gresley's death the LNER did not have a successor in mind to replace him and the board had considered trying to persuade Bulleid away from the Southern Railway where he had moved in 1937. Even though the Southern Railway gave permission for him to leave, Bulleid refused. The board is reputed to have also considered a few younger engineers, J. F. Harrison and Arthur Peppercorn; however, the board decided to appoint Edward Thompson, who was the most senior engineer on the LNER at the time. This was not an unreasonably cautious decision given the prevailing wartime conditions.

Thompson was born in Marlborough, Wiltshire, on 25 June 1881 and was educated at Marlborough College, the same school that Gresley had attended. However, unlike Gresley who decided to gain practical experience at Horwich, Thompson decided to take his academic studies further, studying Mechanical

Science at Pembroke College, Cambridge. Thompson spent time working in both heavy industry and on the railways with Beyer Peacock in Manchester and the Midland Railway in Derby. In 1910 he had become the Assistant Divisional Locomotive Superintendent of the North Eastern Railway. Two years later he moved to the Great Northern Railway after being appointed to the position of Carriage and Wagon Superintendent.

Nearly two decades passed before a move again to become Workshop Manager at Stratford in 1930, his last position before promotion to become Chief Mechanical Engineer of the LNER in 1941. At the time of his promotion Thompson was 60, closer to retirement than some of the board would have liked for a newly appointed CME. However he held the post for five years during the difficult wartime conditions before retiring in 1946.

During Gresley's tenure in office the two engineers were known to disagree on various matters, most notably Gresley's conjugated valve gear. However it seems that Gresley and Thompson shared enough mutual respect to work well together. It is noted on at least two separate occasions Thompson was given

permission by Gresley to look at improving his conjugated valve gear using modern manufacturing and welding techniques that Thompson had experienced in heavy industry. Thompson was also known for being notoriously difficult to deal with at times, disliking others trying to change his ideas or making the case for a different argument.

However, personalities aside, Thompson faced a very different railway to the one Gresley had been designing engines for. The speed and elegance of the Gresley era had been replaced by the need for power, low maintenance and availability to suit the wartime railway. At Thompson's appointment three years of war meant that maintenance pressure brought about by the lack of staff and money was detrimentally low.

Thompson saw the need for a reduced number of locomotive designs carrying out a range of duties, a view at odds with his predecessor who believed engines should be designed to carry out specific jobs. Thompson had proposed reducing the number of individual locomotive classes from over 150 to 19. He also found that in wartime conditions the skilled labour and regular maintenance required by the Gresley Pacifics was not possible and as such the locomotives would suffer and thus affect their availability for traffic and efficient operation.

An area where this was particularly noticeable was the Gresley conjugated gear. Thompson wanted to persuade the LNER board that a departure from the conjugated gear was needed and so he arranged for William Stanier (who delegated the task to E. S. Cox) to compile a report on the gear, detailing the problems encountered and instances of failures, particularly in relation to the middle cylinder, something Thompson ideally wanted to do away with.

The report stated that with the Gresley conjugated gear in a state of total disrepair, as found in some wartime conditions, the centre valve would over-travel at high speeds and the centre cylinder could produce up to 50% more power than the outside cylinders, producing stresses that exceeded the design tolerances for the middle connecting rod big ends. To accompany this a list of failures attributed to the cause were also provided to the board.

Thompson wanted to start building his own fleet of Pacific locomotives to his own designs but in the wartime environment the Board of Directors was unable to release the expenditure on a new untested design as the necessary new

RIGHT Edward
Thompson, Chief
Mechanical Engineer
of the LNER 1941-46.
P2SLC Collection

ABOVE A rare photo
of *Thane of Fife* straight
after rebuilding, complete
with No 995. This number
lasted only a few hours
before being replaced with
the original No 2005.
Ian MacCabe Collection

materials to build new engines could only be authorised by the Ministry of Supply and the Railway Executive Committee.

Thompson, however, persuaded the board that rebuilding locomotives may be an option, promising to keep and reuse as many parts as possible rather than building completely new locomotives, allowing him to carry out his wishes whilst seemingly not needing too many new materials. The six 'P2' locomotives in Scotland became prime candidates for rebuilding as they had been seen by some to be inefficient for the work they eventually settled into or as a complete failure by others due to their repeated failures of axleboxes, crank axles and bearing problems.

On visiting his staff at Edinburgh in May 1942, Thompson informed the Scottish Area officials that he planned to take the engines off their current duties. Some still saw the potential of the 'P2s': E. Windle (Chief Draughtsman) and R. Thom (Mechanical Engineer, Doncaster) both argued with Thompson to replace the swing link control pony truck with one incorporating side control springs to help with the aforementioned breakages and riding issues. This modification had already been carried out on the 'V2' class locomotives after a number of derailments.

However Thompson was keen to rebuild them against their wishes, so much so that he sent Arthur Peppercorn to Edinburgh to quash the resistance to the rebuilding lead by Eric Trask (Locomotive Running Superintendent Edinburgh) and G. Lund (Technical Assistant Scottish Area). As part of the investigations into whether a Pacific with a high tractive effort could carry out the same work as the 'P2s', the unique 'W1' 4-6-4 was sent to Scotland for trials. It seems the engine worked well, coping with the required weight of trains.

Some also voiced their opinion that the engines should have been transferred to work south of the border on heavy wartime trains. However, these ideas fell on deaf ears, possibly because the

opportunity of using them for rebuilding to enable Thompson to experiment with his own ideas was too good to miss. The tests with the rebuilt 'W1' may have made the rebuilding of the 'P2s' inevitable and in October 1942 the board agreed to the rebuilding of one 'P2' engine, which was sent Doncaster for work to begin. This corresponded closely with the last known occurrence of crank axle failure, a failure that some claim brought about the rebuilding program.

An initial outline sketch of the engine appeared in April 1942 showing the leading coupled wheels and pony truck of the original 'P2' replaced by a bogie to create a Pacific. As the Gresley valve gear had caused problems in the wartime environment, and possibly because of his own misgivings about the setup, Thompson decided to fit three independent sets of Walschaerts valve gear incorporating divided drive. Due to wartime conditions Thompson had promised to reuse as many of the original parts as possible so the short connecting rods were reused. This involved placing the cylinders behind the bogie towards the rear of the engine as the clearance between the cylinder backs would be insufficient. The outside cylinders drove the now centre set of coupled wheels.

At the same time Robert Thom commented that the inside connecting rod should also be the same length, something Thompson agreed with as it allowed the valve events of all three cylinders to be as near identical as possible. However, as the middle cylinder drove the front set of driving wheels, the middle cylinder was placed well forward between the frames. The abandonment of the Gresley gear allowed the cut-off to be increased to 75% from the limited 65% of conjugated valve gear engines. The new layout also enabled the piston valves of the inside cylinders to be conventionally placed and the size increased to 10in. However the incorporation of Walschaerts valve gear was not easy as the

arrangement had to be made to fit the existing
frame arrangement but it was soon overcome
and difficulties with reciprocating masses were
resolved. The arrangement was successfully
accommodated and was used without much
alteration on the later Thompson Pacifics.

The boiler was also shortened by nearly two
feet to provide a longer smokebox so that the
chimney would not foul the superheater header.
It was also decided that the live steam pipes
connecting from the superheater header to the
cylinders should be as straight as possible.
Shortening the boiler helped achieve this aim,
although it seems that the far from ideal right-
angle bend of the live steam pipes into the steam
chests was ignored by the designer. The
lengthened smokebox and the set-back cylinders
created a somewhat ungainly appearance to the
locomotive's front end. Further diagrams were
issued showing minor alterations to the design,
including the increase of boiler pressure from
220psi to 225 psi (although no extra work would
be carried out on the boilers).

No 2005 *Thane of Fife* was the engine to be
selected and it was moved to Doncaster where
the conversion was started. The engine's frames
were cut between the first and second pair of
coupled wheels and scrapped. The remaining
sections were transferred to the repair shop ready
for conversion to start in earnest. The streamlined
front casings were also removed and laid up for
scrap, with their nameplates still attached. The
engine emerged from Doncaster works on 16
January 1943 and immediately started running
in turns before being sent to Scotland on 2 April.
After rebuilding the engine was at first known
simply as Class A, with Thompson sending out

instruction on 27 April 1943 amending it to 'A2'.
This was subsequently amended again in August
1945 to 'A2/2' to leave the classification 'A2' ready
for his new fleet of Pacifics.

Thompson reported to the board on 27 July 1943:

'The converted engine has now been in
service for some time and has proved
entirely satisfactory in that it has not only
been able to handle loads at least equal to
the stipulated maximum loading of the P.2
class on the Edinburgh and Aberdeen
section, but has also been remarkably free
from mechanical trouble, so that it has been
consistently available for traffic. It is
proposed that the remaining five P.2 Class
engines should be converted in a similar
way to the 4-6-2 wheel arrangement at an
estimated cost of £2,400 per engine.'

Shortly after in August 1943 the Board gave
permission for the rest of the 'P2' class engines to
be rebuilt at a cost of £12,000. It has also been
reported by contemporary sources that Thompson
was so proud of his rebuilt locomotive that he
sent a photograph to William Stanier with the
note: 'What do you think?', to which he received
no reply.

Work started quickly on the remaining 'P2'
engines with *Wolf of Badenoch* released from the
works in April 1944, *Earl Marischal* in June, *Cock
o' the North* in September and *Mons Meg* and *Lord
President* in November and December respectively.
After rebuilding, all the engines were outshopped
in plain black livery with only 'NE' on the tender,
although some received the full LNER inscription
after the war. No nameplates were fitted to

Nos 2005 and 2006 as the original nameplates were still attached to the now discarded streamlined fronts dumped on the scrap road at Doncaster Works. Eventually, in May 1944, the nameplates were recovered and cleaned up prior to being reunited with the engines at Haymarket. The four other engines received the same livery and nameplates straight after rebuilding.

In June 1944 No 2001 was sent to Cowlairs Works for repaint into full LNER apple green livery prior to its display at Edinburgh as part of an LNER exhibition day. Subsequently, the engines all received apple green livery, some during the LNER reign and others during overhaul or maintenance work after nationalisation, the only major difference being the words 'British Railways' on the tender.

Immediately after rebuilding the engines continued to carry their original numbers 2001-2006 but were later all renumbered during 1946,

being allocated the numbers 501-506. For a very short period in 1948 *Mons Meg* carried an 'E' prefix to its number, designating it as an Eastern Region locomotive, but this was removed shortly afterwards when the engines were, once again, renumbered. This time the numbers allocated were 60501-60506 as part of the British Railways numbering scheme.

A numerical oddity, however, was carried on *Thane of Fife* for just over a fortnight in late April 1946 when the engine received the number 994 prior to gaining its number of 505. This was the only engine to carry a 99x series number in service, which had been assigned to the engines as part of the 1944 renumbering. It was has been noted, however, that No 2005 carried the number 995 on one side for photographic purposes at Doncaster Works, this being immediately removed and replaced by its old number before entry into service.

ABOVE *Wolf of Badenoch* rounds the curve at Inverkeithing with the 2.15pm Edinburgh to Aberdeen express in August 1949.
Ian Allan Library.

BELOW No 60504 stands waiting its next turn of duty.
Ian MacCabe Collection

RIGHT No 60502 *Earl Marischal* **stands at York ready for its next service.**
Ian Allan Library

Returning to Scotland, the engines were split between Aberdeen Ferryhill and Edinburgh Haymarket sheds. Prior to conversion No 2001 was stationed at Aberdeen and No 2002 at Dundee. After rebuilding No 2002 was sent straight to Aberdeen, whilst No 2001 was moved on to Aberdeen after a couple of weeks at Edinburgh Haymarket after rebuilding. Nos 2004/5/6 were all sent straight to Edinburgh after rebuilding. No 2003, however, was loaned to both Gateshead and King's Cross sheds during 1944 and 1945 for comparative trials before joining its classmates at Haymarket.

This engine was measured against 'A4' No 2512 *Silver Fox* and 'A2/1' No 3697 (a member of Thompson's Pacific version of the Gresley 'V2' class produced in 1944), working trains on the East Coast Main Line to Grantham, Doncaster and Leeds. The locomotives on the tests suffered problems with the 'A2/1' and 'A4' being affected by mechanical trouble, resulting in only one test where the figures for each engine could be directly compared whilst working the 1.30pm train from King's Cross to Leeds. The tests showed that No 2003 had the highest coal consumption of 70.5lb per mile compared to the 'A2/1' at 69lb per mile and the 'A4' at 52.3lb per mile.

The tests were repeated a few months later on both passenger and freight workings. On the passenger working the engines ranked in the same order, but on freight working it was found that the 'A2/2' could outperform the 'A4'. The authorities surmised that neither the 'A2/1' nor 'A2/2' needed to work at their maximum capacity and that No 2003's higher coal consumption could be attributed to its larger firebox. Both of Thompson's Pacifics were found to accelerate quicker than the 'A4' due to the formers' smaller

wheel size giving them an advantage. However it seems that Thompson did not use much of the information found from the testing in his development of his Pacifics as although the 'A2/1' seemed to equal the 'A2/2' in the steaming stakes with its smaller firebox, Thompson kept the larger firebox design for his new standard engines.

Officially the engines were allowed to take the same weight trains over the Aberdeen lines as the 'P2s', 530 tons Edinburgh to Aberdeen and 550 tons in the opposite direction. However, when the rebuilt engine arrived back in Scotland to start working trains, the notice about their permissible loads included the following: 'These loads, although similar to the P2 class engine, are the absolute maximum for the A2 class, and trains should be kept within these figures. The figures quoted have application only under the present war-time arrangements and may be subject to further modification of which notification will be advised in course.'

In reality, trains hauled by the engines over the route averaged around 300 tons. On trains above 400 tons footplate crew lodged complaints that the engines became prone to slipping and working the engines became increasingly difficult. This resulted in the local shedmasters rostering 'A4' Pacifics for the heavier trains. This lead to the class working less express passenger work and by 1946 the engines were commonly working in the No 1 Express Goods link hauling fast fish and parcels trains. The Haymarket locomotives also started to stretch their legs further afield, trains south of Edinburgh to Newcastle being worked as common user engines by men from several other depots. With the engines seemingly at home on this work, Nos 60501 and 60502 were transferred from Aberdeen to Edinburgh by September 1949.

However, the class was not without its faults. The engines spent considerable time in Cowlairs Works receiving attention, particularly around the front end of the locomotive where steam pipes, superheaters, exhaust passageways, cylinder and smokebox saddle bolts often fractured or sheared. The required repair work could often not be carried out by shed fitters and required the engines to be sent to Cowlairs for specialist attention which meant spells out of traffic.

During March 1947 these failures lead to the shocking statistic that five out of the six members of the class could be seen out of traffic at Cowlairs Works requiring attention, with only *Lord President* managing to hold the fort as an operating 'A2/2'. The problems were later accounted for by a poor front end design with insufficient support being provided to the frames, allowing them to flex and cause unwanted stresses on the aforementioned components and their fixings. To try to cure the problem a 1in-thick frame support plate was added to the inside of the frames between the centre and outside cylinders whilst the exhaust steam pipes were divided into two sections and fitted with expansion joints to help cure the cracking that often occurred.

The engines also developed a reputation for rough riding, particularly with crews who were more accustomed to the finer riding of Gresley's designs of the pre-war years and not necessarily used to the harder riding engines found elsewhere in the UK. The modifications to the frames made some difference to the locomotives' maintenance needs, especially when allied with close supervision by the shed fitting staff who had become accustomed to the tell-tale signs of an impending problem.

Even so the engines ran poor mileages between general repairs, with No 60501 running the highest figure of 91,301 miles between works visits in September 1954 and August 1956. The engines statistically also spent more time in the workshops than many other classes of the time, with No 2006 being admitted to the works a total of 30 times between 1945 and 1959, compared to only 11 visits by 'A3' *Flying Scotsman* during the same period. The nature of these visits, however, is not fully known for both locomotives so may not be directly comparable.

On 1 July 1946 Arthur Peppercorn succeeded Thompson as the CME of the LNER. At the time of his succession there was still a batch of Thompson standard 'A2' locomotives on order.

ABOVE No 60502 heads a fast freight.
Ian MacCabe Collection

RIGHT No 2005 stands inside Cowlairs shed whilst being weighed.
Ian Allan Library

Peppercorn set about making some changes to the design, reinstating the steam collection on the top of the boiler (previously omitted from some Thompson designs) and moving the cylinders back between the bogie wheels to a more conventional position by using different length connecting rods. The Thompson arrangement of divided drive and the three sets of valve gear were, however, all kept. Attention was also paid to the front end to ensure that problems that manifested on Thompson's Pacifics would not be repeated. The new engines were classified 'A2', with the 'P2' rebuilds reclassified 'A2/2', Thompson 'A2s' being reclassified 'A2/3' and his 'V2' rebuilds becoming 'A2/1'.

After Nationalisation of the railways on 1 January 1948 thoughts turned to how locomotives could best be used across the relevant regions. The new 'A2' and 'A1' class locomotives were found to be ideal for the fast passenger workings on the East Coast Main Line and replaced the 'A2/2' engines on most of this work in Scotland.

On 27 November 1949 Nos 60501, 60502 and 605013 were transferred south of the border to York Shed. New England Shed in Peterborough gained the other three locomotives between November 1949 and January 1950. Like their latter work in Scotland, the engines work was less onerous than in their original form as 'P2s', mainly consisting of fast goods workings or stopping passenger work. The engines were now given the opportunity to spread their legs travelling further afield with the York engines regularly running to London on both passenger and fitted freight workings, along with unusual special workings to Sheffield, Nottingham and Wembley.

The New England engines, likewise, got plenty of use on services north to Newcastle and York and once again south to the capital. For a short period Neville Hill depot in Leeds acquired two 'A2/2' engines, Nos 60501 and 60503, to replace a number of 'A3' class engines

which were out of traffic for repairs. The Leeds men disliked the engines because of their unfamiliarity and tendency to roll and ride badly when pushed at high speeds. During this brief period the engines once again had the opportunity to haul express workings including the down 'North Briton' to York and Newcastle and the up 'Queen of Scots Pullman'.

Although the Neville Hill crews may have disliked the engines, they did get them to perform well. In early 1955 a 365-ton train from York to Leeds covered the 25 miles in 29min 13sec. The maximum speed on the journey was 68mph at Church Fenton and, although it may seem tame by standards of the East Coast Main Line expresses, a performance that an 'A3' would have worked hard to match due to the gradients presented by the route.

Unfortunately, exceptional running like this with light loads over short distances was not always possible. With the engines loaded with heavy trains on longer distance working, the runs were often far more steady and sedate with the locomotives handling their trains in a sure but un-noteworthy manner, including, for a short period in 1954, the 10.10am 'Scotsman' and 10am 'Flying Scotsman' services.

As a small class of engine it was fairly inevitable that the 'A2/2s' would be among the first engines to be withdrawn as part of the modernisation of the railways. Nos 60503 and 60505 were the first to be withdrawn in November 1959 followed in February 1960 by 60501 and 60504 in January 1961. All of the engines were cut up at Doncaster, thus ending the story of the 'P2' and 'A2/2' engines. Only one engine, No 60502 *Earl Marischal*, managed to accumulate more than 1 million miles in service as a 'P2' and 'A2/2', managing a total mileage of 1,034,854. This engine was also the last member of the class in service and was eventually withdrawn on 26 June 1961.

LEFT *Cock o' the North*
awaits scrapping
at Doncaster.
P2SLC Collection

CHAPTER 8

THE MODERN MIKADO

With the scrapping of the rebuilt 'A2/2s', the story of the 'P2' class lay dormant for over half a century. Now 80 years later the prospect of seeing Gresley's express Mikado once again working between Edinburgh and Aberdeen has become a reality with the start of a project to build the seventh member of the 'P2' class.

The story begins 25 years ago with a group of enthusiasts who lamented the complete loss of the Peppercorn 'A1' class steam locomotives and dreamed of constructing a new locomotive.

The rapid onset of dieselisation in the 1960s meant that all the original 49 'A1s' were scrapped, after an average life of only 15 years. There was an attempt to save the last example, No 60145 *Saint Mungo*, but this unfortunately failed and it too was withdrawn in June 1966 and scrapped in September of the same year.

The group decided to turn their dream into a reality and on 17 November 1990 The A1 Steam Locomotive Trust was formally launched. Its aim was simple, to build the 50th member of the 'A1' class and continue the 'A1's evolution by incorporating design improvements that would have occurred had steam motive power continued on the main line railway.

Soon after the trust was founded in 1990 design work started on the new locomotive with the original drawings being sourced to build the new engine. Actual manufacture and construction started in 1994, lasting over a decade until 2008, both at the group's own Darlington Locomotive Works and at specialist engineering firms.

The chosen name for the new locomotive was *Tornado* in honour of the Royal Air Force crews flying in the then recent Gulf War. The locomotive would also eventually carry the 51A shedplate for Darlington and the builder's number 2195. This number was the next in the Darlington Locomotive numbering series and would be accompanied on the worksplate by the final year of completion.

Throughout the construction phase a great deal of behind the scenes work was carried out to support the locomotive. To raise the required funds to build the engine the Trust launched a covenant scheme encouraging the public to donate the price of a pint of beer a week to the locomotive. This would be combined with dedicated donations for components and later a bond issue. The Trust also developed *Tornado* into a brand name, with a selection of merchandise and supporting material once again helping to fund the construction, along with regular appearances of the project on national and regional press and television.

The engine's first steaming, albeit only static, occurred during January 2008 and eventually *Tornado* moved under her own power for the first time on 29 July 2008 at Darlington Locomotive Works. Still in its grey undercoat livery, the engine was publicly launched a few days later on 1 August and then moved to the Great Central Railway in Loughborough to undertake commissioning and running in trials before hauling its first passenger train on 21 September. After faultless running in and accumulating enough miles the engine was transferred to the National Railway Museum at York for its main line testing to begin in early November. After three main line tests the engine gained all the required certification to run on the national network, becoming the newest main line steam locomotive to be built in the UK since *Evening Star* in March 1960. An early Christmas present came on 13 December when the engine was unveiled resplendent in Apple Green livery and soon after was named at a special ceremony by HRH The Prince of Wales and The Duchess of Cornwall before hauling the Royal Train from York Leeds.

Since then the locomotive has run the length and breadth of the UK, accumulating more than 80,000 miles and being seen by hundreds of thousands of people. Seven years after its construction the engine is still as popular as ever and is actively sought for main line railtours and preserved line visits and has even hauled the Royal Train on three occasions.

Not content with building one locomotive the Trust actively sought another project. It had been a long held ambition within the Trust to construct a new Gresley 'P2' locomotive, a popular choice with the A1 team, supporters and enthusiasts.

The engineering and commercial model had been proven with the 'A1' and so it was decided that the group would progress with the construction of a 'P2'. In much the same way that *Tornado* was constructed as the 50 'A1', the new locomotive will become be the seventh member of the 'P2' class and was allocated the next number No 2007. The new 'P2' will be a continuation of the design started by Gresley, incorporating new developments and lessons learnt over the last half a century since the original Mikados were rebuilt. The decision to closely follow the design and style of *Cock o' the North* means that the new locomotive will incorporate the original semi-streamlining and rotary cam valve gear and will look, to all intents and purposes, like No 2001. However, under the skin the locomotive will incorporate a number of

design changes to ensure that any of the previous difficulties or failures sustained by the six engines are removed, in addition to making the new locomotive comply with modern safety and operational standards required by the authorities and Network Rail.

In September 2013 the project to build the engine was launched at The A1 Steam Locomotive Trust's annual supporters' convention, followed by a public event in London in February 2014 to launch the 'P2 for a price of a pint' monthly covenant scheme. The convention also saw the launch of The Founders Club, a fundraising scheme to raise £100,000 from 100 supporters to start the erection of the locomotive's frames. The public launch was followed by a series of events up the East Coast Main Line culminating at Aberdeen. Six months later the Founder's Club had raised a staggering £460,000.

On 14 November 2013, it was announced that the new locomotive would carry the name *Prince of Wales* in honour of HRH The Prince of Wales. The date of the announcement was significant as it was Prince Charles' 65th birthday, with the Trust being granted Royal consent from HM The Queen shortly beforehand. The name, however, was not new to the LNER. One of Gresley's 'A3' Pacifics, No 2553, had previously carried the name after being named by the then Prince of Wales on a visit to Doncaster Works on 11 November 1926. The name had also been carried on a Great Central Railway 'D11' class that was absorbed into the LNER during the

Grouping. The name is a departure from the theme of names carried by the original 'P2s' that are all based around Scottish folklore. Respecting this the Trust has sought approval from the Royal Household to use the Scottish version of the title, 'Duke of Rothesay', when the locomotive visits Scotland and at other select occasions. This name was also used on another Class A2/1 LNER locomotive built in 1944.

Behind the scenes work on the project had started long before the launch event. Firstly, the original London & North Eastern Railway drawings were digitally scanned from the collections at the National Railway Museum.

These drawings gave the project engineers the starting point to design an improved 'P2' locomotive. A feasibility study was also carried out to examine the commercial, engineering and certification challenges that building a new 'P2' would face as, without knowing whether the project could be successfully accepted to run on the current main line, the huge cost of building the locomotive could not be justified. Additionally the Office of Rail and Road was consulted as it holds the ultimate authority to operate trains and after negotiations it confirmed that it had no objections to the project and would continue to support the new locomotive.

The original engines had a reputation for derailing and being hard riding on curved track. The Trust examined the historical evidence and found that, whilst most of the rumours were unsubstantiated, there were some known occasions of faults. The engineers spent some time looking at the problem, including the LNER's swing-link pony trucks. Various other locomotive classes had been fitted with these but were later converted to use the later style 'V2' class pony truck introduced in 1936. Some of the 'V2' class had shown a tendency to derail and the LNER redesigned the truck to overcome this problem, rolling it out as a standard fitting on other classes. However, for some reason the original six 'P2' engines did not get this modification, possibly because of their distance from Doncaster Works or due to their small class size. The Trust's engineers came to the conclusion

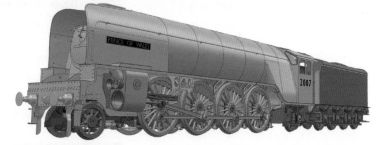

that the later 'V2' pony truck should solve all the problems of the original 'P2s'; however, for this to be accepted on the modern railway the design had to be proved before the engine was built. Derby based Delta Rail was consulted and used its industry-recognised VAMPIRE computer modelling software to re-evaluate the design. Although normally used for modern traction the system lent itself to the problem at hand and had been used as part of the approvals process for 'A1' *Tornado*.

As a test to determine the reliability of using a computer program, a 3D model of *Tornado* was produced from technical drawings and put to the test. This was then compared to real data collected when the locomotive was tested at the Great Central Railway as part of its certification process. The details matched, proving that the computer system could accurately predict how a steam locomotive would behave on the railway. Next, the original drawings of *Cock o' the North* were used to build a 3D model and then subjected to rigorous testing. The results showed that on

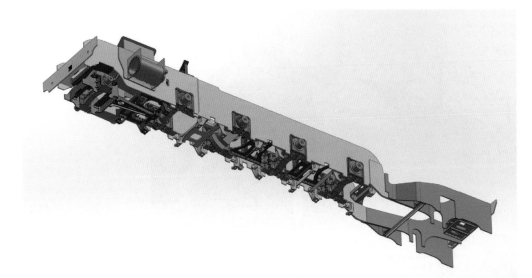

LEFT CAD drawing of No 2007 showing the detail of the frames, axles and associated fittings, stretchers and modified front pony truck. *P2SLC Collection*

extremely tight curves the design of the original swing-link pony truck lead to the front-coupled wheelsets being slightly lifted from the rail, allowing for possible derailments. However, this only presented itself on the tightest curves not commonly found on the main line but perhaps helps explain the issues on tight curves in poorly maintained depots. Finally, a 3D model was produced of the proposed design with the later 'V2'-style pony truck incorporated. After testing it was found that the modification solved the problem of the lifted wheelsets and allowed the locomotive to negotiate tight corners. The software also showed that the locomotive's riding characteristics would be somewhere near that of *Tornado*, much to the satisfaction of the engineers, and possibly superior when running on favourably aligned track

Bearing and crank axle failures were also investigated. Technology has moved on since the introduction of the original engines over 70 years ago and helped the Trust's engineers devise solutions to overcome these problems. New designs were drawn up incorporating stress relieving grooves and other details that complied with the BR BAS 504 design principles, the nationally recognised standards for axles. Once again computer studies were carried out to confirm that the design changes will perform as expected. With the two make or break major design problems resolved the Trust started detailed design work on the locomotive, ready to start construction. From the outset the engine would be designed in 3D CAD. This allows detailed work like pipe runs and electronic cable runs to be designed into the locomotive from the beginning. The decision was also made to use as

ABOVE The newly cast wheels at Darlington Locomotive Works awaiting the delivery of tyres and axles. *David Elliot*

much of *Tornado's* design and components so that as far as reasonably practicable the two engines would have interchangeable parts, whilst also keeping the cost of patterns and certification down. The original drawings show that the two locomotive designs share many smaller components as well as certain larger items.

The frames for the engine mostly followed the original design with some modifications to the front to incorporate the new design of pony truck, whilst the rear of the frames were modified to copy the arrangement of Cartazzi trailing truck fitted to *Tornado*. Subsequent to this decision it was found that the last four 'P2s' already had this modification incorporated into their manufacture. The frame stretchers also required some modification from the originals so that air braking and other components could be fitted. The locomotive would also be fitted with roller bearings throughout on its wheelsets, again following the design of No 60163 *Tornado*, to aid maintenance and reliability.

ABOVE LEFT The frames for *Prince of Wales* at Darlington Locomotive Works. *Bob Hughes*

ABOVE RIGHT The frames and footplate for No 2007 viewed from the cab end of the locomotive. *David Elliot*

The plan to base the aesthetics of No 2007 on *Cock o' the North* means that a rotary valve gear is preferable for the new engine rather than Walschaerts valve gear as on the other 'P2s'. Some changes may be made to the proportions of the cylinders to compensate for the increased boiler pressure available from the 250lb/sq in diagram 118A fitted to *Tornado* as opposed to the 220lb/sq in diagram 106 boiler fitted to the original locomotive. However, the Lentz gear used on *Cock o' the North* after it was fitted with stepped cams offered only limited cut-off settings which may have contributed in part to No 2001's high coal consumption. The Trust was keen to use the original Lentz infinitely variable rotary cam gear on No 2007 to give unlimited control of the cut-off; however, this posed a problem for the Trust as no drawings could be found. When the drawing register for the original engine was consulted it was found that the LNER had no drawings for the Lentz valve gear because it was supplied under licence to Associated Locomotive Equipment Limited, who provided the original equipment to the LNER. Various archives in the UK were consulted but no trace of the original drawings has been found. When the licence ran out in the 1940s, the American firm The Franklin Railway Supply Company (a subsidiary of Lima Locomotive Works) carried on the development of the rotary valve gear, eventually being granted a patent known under the name of Franklin Valve Gear. After several months of research, assisted by George Carpenter in the UK and the family of Vernon Smith in the USA, the Trust acquired the original blue prints for a Santa Fe 4-8-4 locomotive fitted with the Franklin gear. Further insight came from combining the information from the USA with a set of drawings for a Lentz fitted South African Railways '15E'

locomotive (of similar proportions to the new 'P2'). This has assisted the Trust to start developing plans to incorporate the Lentz/Franklin gear into *Prince of Wales* whilst also taking the opportunity to revisit the known problem of clearance volumes within the cylinders.

The original locomotives were fitted with a diagram 106 boiler. These boilers share a genetic link to the 118A boiler fitted to *Tornado*. All the principal dimensions are the same apart from the boiler barrel which on the 'A1' is fractionally shorter. The pressure on the 118A boiler was also higher at 250lb/sq in, compared to the 220 lb/sq in of the original, whilst the later boiler also had a larger combustion chamber as fitted to *Wolf of Badenoch*. As interchangability of components and standardisation between the 'A1' and 'P2' were important to the Trust the decision was taken to design an identical boiler to *Tornado* into the new 'P2'. This would mean enlarging the length of the smokebox to account for the shorter barrel. However, aesthetically this would be hidden under the cladding and not noticeable, whilst also allowing greater space in the smokebox for modern spark arresting equipment. The locomotive will have Davies-Metcalfe pattern injectors similar to *Tornado* rather than a feed water heater and one injector.

The tender will be nearly identical to that used by *Tornado*, featuring the modifications that allow more water and slightly less coal to be carried to allow for longer distances of main line running without stopping for fuel. As per the original 'P2' tender, it will ride on spoked wheels which were also used on some of the original 'A1' class along with *Tornado*. Again, roller bearings will be used to reduce rolling resistance and reduce maintenance. Like *Tornado* extra cabinets

RIGHT James May constructing the first component for the new locomotive. *Andy Hardy*

LEFT The finished smokebox door dart. *Andy Hardy*

BELOW Tim and Ben Godfrey, Sir Nigel Gresley's grandsons, pressing the button to start the cutting of the frames for *Prince of Wales*. *Andy Hardy*

will be fitted onto the tender front to house the electronics required for the engine.

Braking for *Prince of Wales* will follow the design perfected during the construction of No 60163, primary air brakes for locomotive and train with secondary vacuum brakes for working heritage rolling stock. The electrical system will be similar to that fitted to *Tornado* and will feature all the required systems for the engine to work on the main line. The original 'P2s' were not equipped with any electrical equipment or lighting but with careful redesign it has been possible to incorporate the required needs without detracting from the aesthetic look of the original locomotive.

With the initial work underway it can be seen that the 'P2' project already has a head start with the vast number of common components the locomotive shares with *Tornado*, many patterns for which are held by the Trust. It is estimated that there is approximately 70% commonality with the Peppercorn Class A1 ranging from the entire tender, boiler, including all the fittings, rear Cartazzi assembly, braking system and all roller bearing components to many individual parts of the frame structure and the electronic systems.

However, progress can only move forward when there is the financial basis to support the project. With an estimated cost of £5 million needed to complete the locomotive the Trust has to work hard to secure the funds. Unlike heritage restorations, the project is not eligible for Heritage Lottery Funding or other similar historical grants. This led the Trust to develop the Covenantor's scheme, with people giving a small amount of money on a regular basis to help construct the engine. With *Tornado*, around 1500 individuals donate on a monthly basis which helped to construct and helps with the operation of the locomotive. *Prince of Wales* is being funded with the same model and the Covenantors receive benefits in return for their

ABOVE Frame cutting for the new locomotive in action. *Andy Hardy*

support. It is hoped that many who have supported *Tornado* will support *Prince of Wales* and that they will be joined by new supporters who wish to see a new 'P2'. This will be supplemented by a Dedicated Donations scheme, allowing supporters the opportunity to sponsor specific components on the locomotive along with sponsorship from commercial organisations of materials and labour. Since the formal launch of the project in February 2014 the Trust has

ABOVE LEFT New castings delivered to Darlington ready for machining. *David Elliot*

ABOVE RIGHT The newly pressed smokebox door. *David Elliot*

raised over £2 million in pledges to construct *Prince of Wales*.

With the project underway the Trust wanted a high profile way to reach the masses and tell them about their new project. In February 2014 the TV presenter, media celebrity and self-confessed steam enthusiast James May agreed to make the first component of what will be the most powerful steam locomotive to operate in Great Britain. James was already familiar with the Trust's work after *Tornado* appeared on the television programme *Top Gear* in 2009 and had also travelled on the locomotive on other occasions and developed an interest in the 'P2' project when the idea was first mooted so was more than happy to help the Trust kick-start the new engine. James applied his engineering prowess in crafting *Prince of Wales's* smoke box door dart, the component at the front of the locomotive that secures the smoke box door shut. At Darlington Locomotive Works, James set to work turning a drawing and some pieces of steel into the first component. During the day the national and local press visited the works to watch him at work. The Trust also embraced social media and when the component was completed James shared it with thousands of his followers around the world.

With fundraising and marketing off to a good start the locomotive's mainframes were rolled on 23 April 2014. This was followed by the profiling of the frames at Tata Steel in Scunthorpe. The profiling was carried out by a CNC machine direct from the CAD drawings with command to start the operation given jointly by Gresley's grandsons Tim and Ben Godfrey. Shortly after the frames were cut they were taken to the Borough Foundry in Middlesbrough to be machined before delivery to Darlington Locomotive Works. With the frames at Darlington the opportunity was taken to temporarily assemble them with stretcher bars for a special Supporter's Day in June 2014. At the same time various other parts

were ordered as the fundraising allowed. All 20 wheels were cast by the Trust's principal sponsor William Cook Cast Products before being sent for proof machining. To accompany these the wheel tyres, axles and crankpins were also ordered.

Once the design work on the new frame stretchers was completed the first batch of cast components was ordered. The patterns for most of these components were produced by a CNC machine from polystyrene direct from the CAD drawings, helping to keep costs down and create a shorter production time in comparison to handmade wooden patterns. Alongside the frame stretchers over 60 other components such as the hornblocks, buffer casings and frame brackets were also cast. Many of these castings were sent straight for machining before being stored at Darlington ready for assembly when needed. To fit many of these parts together over 1,000 fitted bolts have been ordered.

Another major order was placed for roller bearings. The bearings are identical to those used on *Tornado* and were ordered early in the construction process to ensure that their long manufacturing lead time would not inhibit progress on the project.

In July 2015 The Gresley Society Trust joined the list of sponsors for No 2007 by offering to sponsor the face of the new engine. The Gresley Society Trust was established in 1963 to sustain the legacy of Sir Nigel Gresley and saw the construction and development of Gresley's express Mikado as an opportunity to educate and demonstrate Gresley's work.

The sponsorship by The Gresley Society Trust includes:

• Design changes, rolling and assembly of smokebox barrel
• Smokebox/boiler and smokebox front rings
• Smokebox door and most fittings (hinges, dart, etc)

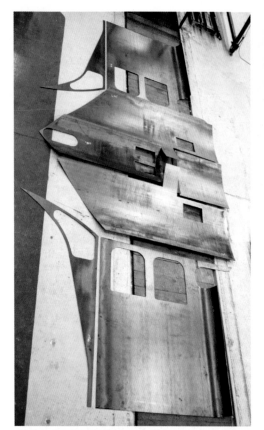

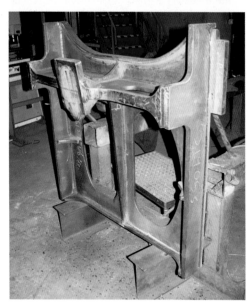

TOP LEFT The flat-pack laser-cut cab components laid out ready for assembly. *David Elliot*

TOP RIGHT The cab assembly is trial fitted to the frames. *David Elliot*

BOTTOM LEFT The fabricated combined frame stay and motion bracket. *David Elliot*

BOTTOM RIGHT The three leading coupled axlebox hornblocks are trial fitted. *David Elliot*

- Cross bar, ribs and crinolines
- Chimney pattern and machining
- Fairing around chimney and smoke lifting sheets
- Whistle bracket, most handrails and knobs

With the components sponsored, work immediately started on the smokebox. The most complicated part (owing to its shape), the smokebox door was completed soon after at South Devon Railway Engineering. The door was a single pressing and required the firm to make both a male and female press tool as part of the contract. The finished component was then delivered to Darlington Locomotive Works for machining and the fitting of the smokebox door dart previously made by James May a year earlier.

To accompany the smokebox the Trust ordered the locomotive's distinctive cab. The parts will be cut and profiled before delivery to Darlington for final assembly and fitting to the locomotive. It is hoped that by the end of 2016 the locomotive will be taking shape with the locomotive on its wheels, complete with cab and smokebox, giving its supporters, enthusiasts and the public a chance to see the elegant lines of *Prince of Wales* taking shape.

Subject to fundraising, it is planned to have the locomotive finished by 2021. Once complete the locomotive will be certified to operate on the main line by Network Rail and therefore, subject to some weight and other restrictions, will be able to operate throughout Great Britain on the main line hauling railtours and other charter trains along with visiting main-line connected Heritage Railways.

No 2007 is not, however, the only 'P2' under construction as for over a decade a small group of like-minded people, primarily based in Doncaster, South Yorkshire, have been quietly working towards their goal of re-creating a 'P2'.

The Doncaster P2 Locomotive Trust was formed to build a replica of No 2001 *Cock o' the North*. Unlike *Prince of Wales*, the group have decided to recreate a streamlined 'P2'. This decision was taken due to the perceived issues with the original design of No 2001. During the early part of 2014 the locomotive's frames were cut at Tata Steel, Scunthorpe, before being sent for bending and profiling. By the autumn of 2014 the frame components had been delivered to Didcot Railway Centre for display prior to assembly. Since then work has focused on producing further drawings and CAD work and the slow task of fundraising.

APPENDIX 1

No 2001
Cock o' the North
Works Number: 1789

22 May 1934	Engine completed at Doncaster Works with Rotary Cam Poppet Valve gear, ACFI feedwater heater. Painted in Apple Green livery and numbered No 2001. Allocated to Doncaster depot.
1 June	Unveiled at King's Cross press day.
31 July 1934	Allocated to Edinburgh Haymarket depot.
27 August 1934	Tablet exchange apparatus fitted.
24 November 1934	Scroll cams replaced by stepped cams.
5 December 1934	Engine Travels to Vitry, France.
21 February 1935	Engine returns to England. Allocated to Haymarket depot.
30 March 1935	Oil cooling system fitted to valve gear.
30 September 1937	Withdrawn for rebuilding as streamlined engine.
14 April 1938	Rebuilt engine with piston valves and full streamlining. ACFI equipment removed.
24 June 1944	Withdrawn pending rebuilding as Pacific.
14 September 1944	Rebuilding as Pacific completed. Finished in wartime black livery.
29 October 1944	Allocated to Aberdeen Ferryhill depot.
11 August 1946	Engine repainted in Apple Green livery at Cowlairs
12 November 1946	Renumbered 501.
22 May 1948	Renumbered 60501.
4 September 1949	Allocated to Haymarket depot.
27 November 1949	Allocated to York depot.
21 February 1950	Repainted in BR green livery.
27 November 1950	Allocated to Neville Hill depot, Leeds.
17 December 1950	Allocated to York depot.
22 January 1960	Withdrawn from service.
8 February 1960	Cut-up at Doncaster Works
Lifetime mileage	978,597 miles. (125,670 with Poppet Valves, 362,136 as a Mikado, 616,461 as a Pacific).

No 2002
Earl Marischal
Works Number: 1796

6 October 1934	Engine completed at Doncaster with piston valves and Walschaerts valve gear. Painted in Apple Green livery and numbered No 2002. Allocated to Doncaster depot.
17 April 1935	Additional smoke lifting plates fitted.
9 June 1935	Allocated to Edinburgh Haymarket depot.
22 June 1935	Allocated to Dundee Tay Bridge depot.
14 October 1936	Rebuilt with fully streamlined front end. Allocated to Aberdeen Ferryhill.
1 April 1944	Withdrawn pending rebuilding as Pacific.
23 June 1944	Rebuilding as Pacific completed. Finished in wartime black livery.
12 May 1946	Renumbered 502.
29 March 1947	Engine repainted in Apple Green livery at Cowlairs
30 June 1948	Renumbered 60502.
4 September 1949	Allocated to Edinburgh Haymarket.
27 November 1949	Allocated to York depot.
7 March 1951	Repainted in BR green livery.
26 June 1961	Withdrawn from service.
3 July 1961	Cut-up at Doncaster Works.
Lifetime mileage	1,034,854 miles. (360,907 as a Mikado, 673,947 as a Pacific.)

No 2003
Lord President
Works Number: 1836

13 June 1936	Completed as fully streamlined engine with piston valves. Painted in Apple Green livery and numbered No 2003. Allocated to Edinburgh Haymarket depot.
4 September 1936	Allocated to Dundee Tay Bridge depot.
23 October 1942	Allocated to Edinburgh Haymarket depot.
27 November 1942	Allocated to NE area.
20 March 1944	Allocated to Edinburgh Haymarket.
2 September 1944	Withdrawn pending rebuilding as Pacific.
17 December 1944	Rebuilding as Pacific completed. Finished in wartime black livery. Allocated to King's Cross depot.

2 February 1944	Allocated to Gateshead depot.
20 March 1945	Allocated to Haymarket depot.
11 April 1945	Allocated to King's Cross depot
13 May 1945	Allocated to Edinburgh Haymarket depot.
30 June 1946	Renumbered 503.
21 December 1946.	Engine repainted in Apple Green livery at Cowlairs
17 May 1948	Allocated to Aberdeen Ferryhill depot.
26 May 1948	Allocated to Edinburgh Haymarket depot.
18 September 1948.	Renumbered 60503.
27 November 1949	Allocated to York depot.
31 August 1950	Repainted in BR green livery.
27 November 1950	Allocated to Neville Hill depot, Leeds.
17 December 1950	Allocated to York depot.
27 November 1959	Withdrawn from service and cut-up.
Lifetime mileage	754,781 miles. (246,283 as a Mikado, 508,498 as a Pacific).

No 2004
Mons Meg
Works Number: 1839.

11 July 1936	Completed as fully streamlined engine with piston valve and exhaust steam bypass valve. Painted in Apple Green livery and numbered No 2004. Allocated to Edinburgh Haymarket depot.
1 July 1937	Bypass valve modified.
1 June 1939	Bypass valve modified.
22 August 1944	Withdrawn pending rebuilding as Pacific.
3 November 1944	Rebuilding as Pacific completed. Finished in wartime black livery.
30 June 1946.	Renumbered 504
12 March 1948.	Renumbered E504.
23 March 1948	Renumbered 60504 and painted in Apple Green livery.
9 January 1950	Allocated to New England depot, Peterborough.
26 May 1950	Repainted in BR green livery.
23 January 1961	Withdrawn from service and cut-up
Lifetime mileage	989,040 miles. (294,243 as a Mikado, 694,797 as a Pacific).

No 2005
Thane of Fife
Works Number: 1840

11 July 1936	Completed as fully streamlined engine with piston valve and single blastpipe and chimney. Painted in Apple Green livery and numbered No 2005. Allocated to Dundee Tay Bridge depot.
26 October 1942	Withdrawn pending rebuilding as Pacific.
18 January 1943	Rebuilding as Pacific completed. Finished in wartime black livery.
3 April 1943	Allocated to Edinburgh Haymarket depot.
25 April 1946	Renumbered 994.
12 May 1946	Renumbered 505.
5 June 1948	Renumbered 60505 and repainted Apple Green.
30 December 1949	Allocated to New England depot, Peterborough.
4 January 1952	Repainted in BR green livery.
10 November 1959	Withdrawn from service and cut-up.
Lifetime mileage	919,747 miles. (246,283 as a Mikado, 673,464 as a Pacific).

No 2006
Wolf of Badenoch
Works Number: 1842

5 September 1936	Completed as fully streamlined engine with piston valve and larger firebox combustion chamber. Painted in Apple Green livery and numbered No 2006. Allocated to Edinburgh Haymarket depot.
16 November 1936	Allocated to Aberdeen Ferryhill depot.
23 October 1942	Allocated to Edinburgh Haymarket depot.
28 January 1944	Withdrawn pending rebuilding as Pacific.
15 April 1944	Rebuilding as Pacific completed. Finished in wartime black livery.
30 June 1946	Renumbered 506.
18 October 1947	Painted in Apple Green livery.
18 December 1948	Renumbered 60506.
8 April 1949	Allocated to Aberdeen Ferryhill depot.
15 May 1949	Allocated to Edinburgh Haymarket depot.
20 November 1949	Allocated to New England depot, Peterborough.
28 July 1950	Repainted in BR green livery.
4 April 1961	Withdrawn from service and cut-up.
Lifetime mileage	916,200 miles. (287,187 as a Mikado, 629,013 as a Pacific).

APPENDIX 2

Locomotive diagrams as issued by the LNER CME department charting the design, construction and rebuilding of the 'P2' and 'A2/2' Class.

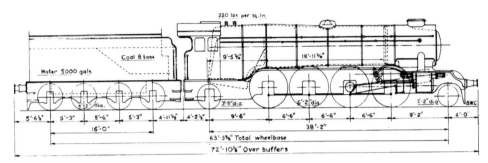

Proposed 2-8-2 Type March 1932

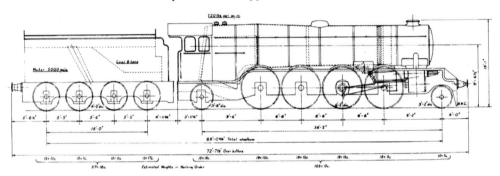

Proposed 2-8-2 Type April 1932

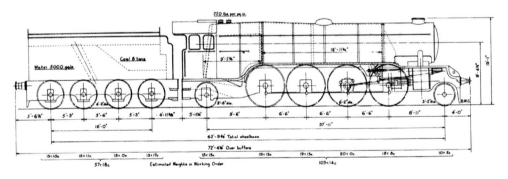

Proposed P2 Class January 1933

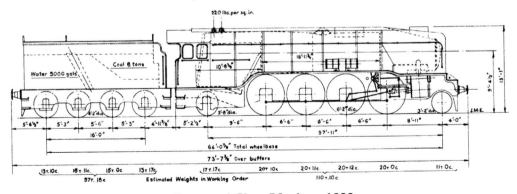

Proposed Class P2 - June 1933

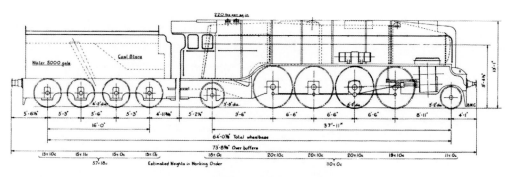

Proposed Class P2 July 1933

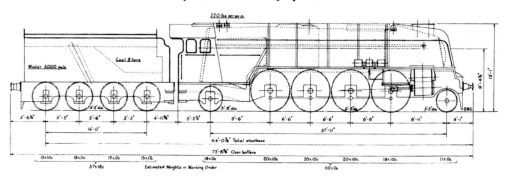

Proposed Class P2 October 1933

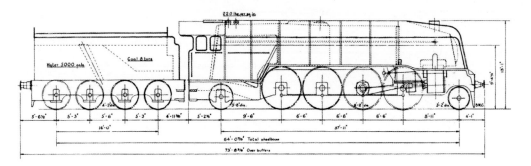

Proposed P2 Class October 1933

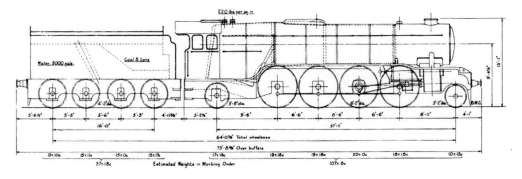

Proposed Class P2 - December 1933

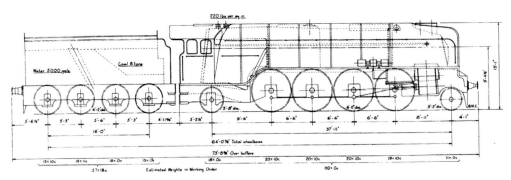

Proposed Class P2 March 1934

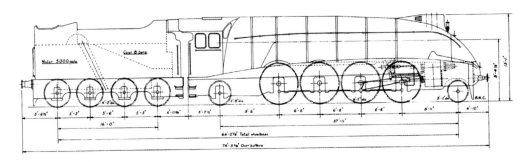

Proposed Class P2 March 1936

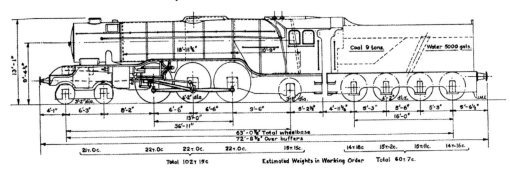

Proposed 4-6-2 Type A - April 1942

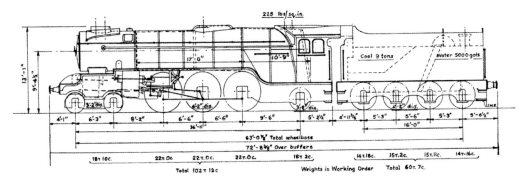

Class A - Rebuilt January 1943 (Became A2/2)

APPENDIX 3

Table of comparative sizes and statistics for locomotives mentioned.

	O2	A3 (1927 batch)	P1 (No. 2393 as built)	P2 (No.2001 as built)	P2 (No.2002 as built)	P2 (No.2003-5)	P2 (No.2006)	A2/2	PeppercornA1
Cylinders	3	3	3	3	3	3	3	3	3
Cylinder size	18.5" x 26"	19" x 26"	20" x 26"	21" x 26"	21" x 26"	21" x 26"	21" x 26"	20" x 26"	19" x 26"
Motion	Walschaerts	Walschaerts	Walschaerts	Lentz Rotary Cam	Walschaerts	Walschaerts	Walschaerts	Walschaerts	Walschaerts
Boiler:									
Max. diam	5'6"	6'5"	6'5"	6'5"	6'5"	6'5"	6'5"	6'5"	6'5"
Distance between tubeplates	14' 1.5"	18' 11.75"	19' 0"	18' 11.75"	18' 11.75"	18' 11.75"	17' 11.75"	17' 0"	16' 11.5"
Firebox Length	10' 1.5"	9' 5.75"	9' 5.5"	10'9"	10'9"	10'9"	11'9"	10'9"	11'4"
Pitch	8' 7.25"	9' 4.5"	9' 4.5"	9' 4.5"	9' 4.5"	9' 4.5"	9' 4.5"	9' 4.5"	9' 4.5"
Diagram	100A	94HP/94A	94		106	106	106A	108	118
Heating Surface:									
Firebox	168 sq. ft.	215 sq.ft.	215 sq.ft.	237 sq.ft.	237 sq.ft.	237 sq.ft.	252.5 sq.ft.	237 sq.ft.	245.3 sq.ft.
Tubes	1048 sq. ft.	1398.8 sq.ft.	1880 sq.ft.	1354.2 sq.ft.	1354.2 sq.ft.	1354.2 sq.ft.	1281.4 sq.ft.	1211.57 sq.ft	1211.57 sq.ft.
Flues	460 sq. ft.	1122 sq.ft.	835 sq.ft.	1122.8sq.ft	1122.8sq.ft	1122.8sq.ft	1063.7 sq.ft	1004.5sq.ft	1004.50 sq.ft.
Total Evaporative	1676 sq.ft.	2736 sq.ft.	29300 sq.ft.	2714.0 sq.ft.	2714.0 sq.ft.	2714.0 sq.ft.	2597.6 sq.ft	2453.07 sq.ft.	2461.37 sq.ft.
Superheater	344 sq. ft	706 sq.ft.	525 sq.ft	776.5 sq.ft.	776.5 sq.ft.	776.5 sq.ft.	748.9 sq.ft	679.67 sq.ft	679.67 sq.ft
Total	2020 sq. ft.	3442.6 sq.ft.	3455 sq.ft.	3940.5 sq.ft.	3940.5 sq.ft.	3940.5 sq.ft.	3346.5 sq.ft	3132.74 sq.ft	3141.04 sq.ft
Grate Area	27.9 sq.ft.	41.25 sq.ft.	41.25 sq.ft.	50 sq.ft.	50 sq.ft.	50 sq.ft.	50 sq.ft.	50 sq.ft.	50 sq.ft.
Boiler Pressure	180 lb./sq.in.	220 lb/sq.in.	180 lb./sq.in.	220 lb/sq.in.	220 lb/sq.in.	220 lb/sq.in.	220 lb/sq.in.	225 lb/sq.in.	250 lb/sq.in.
Leading Wheels	2' 8"	3' 2"	3' 2"	3' 2"	3' 2"	3' 2"	3' 2"	3' 2"	3' 2"
Coupled Wheels	4' 8"	6' 8"	5' 2"	6' 8"	6' 8"	6' 8"	6' 8"	6' 2"	6' 8"
Trailing Wheels	NA	3' 8"	3' 8"	3' 8"	3' 8"	3' 8"	3' 8"	3' 8"	3' 8"
Tender Wheels	3' 9"	4' 2"	3' 9"	4' 2"	4' 2"	4' 2"	4' 2"	4' 2"	4' 2"
Tractive Effort (at 85%)	36,470 lb.	32,909 lb.	38,500 lb. (with booster)	43,462 lb.	43,462 lb.	43,462 lb.	43,462 lb.	40,318 lb.	37, 397 lb.
Length over buffers	63' 3"	70' 5"	69' 10"	73' 8.5"	73' 8.5"	73' 8.5"	73' 8.5"	72' 8.5"	72' 11.75"
Wheelbase:									
Engine	27' 2"	35' 9"	36' 2"	37' 11"	37' 11"	37' 11"	37' 11"	36' 11"	36' 3"
Tender	13' 6"	16' 0"	13' 0"	16' 0"	16' 0"	16' 0"	16' 0"	16' 0"	16' 0"
Total	53' 3"	60' 10.5"	69' 8"	64' 1"	64' 1"	64' 1"	64' 1"	63' 1"	62' 5.25"
Weight (full):									
Engine	75t 16c	96t 5c	100t 0c	110t 5c	109t 8c	107t 3c	107t 3c	101t 10c	104t 2c
Tender	51t 10c	57t 18c	51t 8c	55t 6c	57t 18c	60t 7c	60t 7c	60t 7c	60t 7c
Adhesive	67t 7c	66t 2c	71 t 10 c (booster 18t 4c)	80t 12c	80t 10c	78t 19c	78t 19c	66t 0c	66t 0c
Max. axle load	17t 12c	22t 1c	18t 13c	20t 10c	20t 14c	20t 0c	20t 0c	22t 0c	22t 0c
Water Capacity	4,200 gallons	5,000 gallons	4,700 gallons	5,000 gallons	5,000 gallons	5,000 gallons	5,000 gallons	5,000 gallons	5,000 gallons
Coal Capacity	7t 10c	8t 0c	7t 0c	8t 0c	8t 0c	8t 0c	8t 0c	9t 0c	9t 0c

APPENDIX 4

The following is a transcript taken from a diary of one of the LNER engineers, possibly E Windle, Doncaster Chief Draughtsman, who was present during the testing of *Cock o' the North* at the Vitry locomotive testing station.

DIARY OF TRIALS IN FRANCE
ENGINE NO 2001 – '*COCK O' THE NORTH*'
1934

Wednesday December 5
The locomotive, together with three 40-ton wagons loaded with Yorkshire Main coal, a covered goods van containing spares for the locomotive, and a 20-ton brake van were placed on the train ferry at 6.15 p.m. The voyage over to Calais commenced at 8.30 p.m.

Thursday December 6
The train ferry was berthed at Calais at 8.20 a.m., but owing to Customs formalities it was not until 12.30 p.m. that the train was disembarked. There was some difficulty with the Customs authorities regarding the spare parts, and if in future any rolling stock or spares are sent over, it must be arranged that they stand at least 24 hours at Calais for Customs purposes. The engine was lighted up and proceeded to Calais Locomotive Depot at 5.45 p.m. and remained there throughout the night.

Friday December 7
The engine left Calais Maritime for Vitry at 7.36 a.m. and travelled via Amiens, Montdidier, Le Bourget, Villeneuve St. Georges, Juvisy and Ivry. It arrived at the testing plant at Vitry at 6.30 p.m.

Saturday December 8
The brakes of the testing plant were set to suit our wheelbase and the engine was run on the testing plant for the first time at 5.0p.m. It ran on to the test bed under its own steam.

Sunday December 9
During the whole of the morning the engine was at the disposal of the representatives of the publication *L'illustration* for photographic purposes.

Monday December 10 to Wednesday December 12
The engine was fitted up with the necessary pyrometers and water meters. The connections provided in the smokebox sides prove to be unsuitable for the O.C.E.H. pyrometers and they put on new fittings of their own make. Additional fittings were also required in the manifold under the L.H. footstep for the smokebox vacuum and the back pressure in the exhaust passage.

Thursday December 13
The engine ran on the test bed for the first time. In the morning it was run lightly to see everything was in order, but in the afternoon it was run up to a speed of 76 miles per hour to enable the cinematograph trade to obtain films of the engine in motion. The engine was not riding evenly on the rollers, and while the frame remained central on the wheels, particularly the driving wheels moved over towards the right, the inside of the R.H. tyre binding hard on the rail of the plant. Towards the end of the afternoon the R.H. driving axlebox was observed to be running warm. On inspection the axlebox tray it was found that a considerable amount of the metal was melted out, and arrangements were made for the engine to be taken into the electric locomotive shops of the Paris Orleans Railway at Vitry where a suitable wheel drop is installed. An examination of the plant after the engine had been removed showed, by the marks on the L.H. rail, that similar difficulty regarding the moving over the wheels to the right had been experienced with other engines.

Friday December 14

At 6.30 a.m. the engine was taken to the Paris Orleans Works about a mile from the testing plant. The driving wheels were dropped and the axleboxes dismantled. Both R.H. and L.H. boxes were badly pounded on the back against the face of the horn, the L.H. box being rather the worse of the two. Two new boxes brought out from Doncaster were therefore fitted. The Journals were indifferent condition. Whilst the driving wheels were dismantled opportunity was taken to grind off the corner on the inside of the tyre where the change of width from 4'-5⅝" to 4'-5⅞" takes place.

Saturday December 15 and Sunday December 16

The work on refitting the boxes and re-erecting the wheels, rods, etc was completed in the early afternoon of Sunday, and the engine again arrived at the plant about 5.30 p.m. It was put on to the test plant and run lightly for about 2½ hours.

Monday December 17

The engine was run light throughout the morning. Since fitting the new boxes to the driving wheels the effect of the side movement has been transferred to the leading and trailing wheels, the root of the flange of the R.H. trailing wheels in particular binding hard on the radius of the R.H. roller of the plant. In the afternoon a series of tests were carried out at 60 Kilometres per hour at 12, 18, 25 and 35% cut off with the blast pipe as when the engine left Doncaster, that is, 6" diameter and with the No 0, the smallest vee bars. There was considerable smoke at the 12% and 18% cut offs, and at these low cut offs the fire was somewhat sluggish. At 12 and 18% cut off positions there was no exhaust pressure registered on the gauge. The pipe was coupled to the front of the blast pipe immediately under the blast pipe top joint. The position of this coupling was now altered to the exhaust passage in the cylinder casting immediately above the exhaust valve. The beat at the chimney top was irregular, especially at the low speeds. The engine returned to the Shed in good order.

Tuesday December 18

The engine was put on the plant at 9.0 a.m. with the object carrying out test at 60 Kilometres per hour and at 45 cut off. After 20 minutes running, however, in order to bring the conditions up to test requirements, it was apparent that the L.H. crank pin was running hot. The engine returned to the Shed at 12.0 mid-day and the remainder of the day was occupied in fitting a new bush which had been brought out from Doncaster.

Wednesday December 19

In order to run in the new coupling rod bush, the morning's work commenced with a run of 15 minutes duration, with but little resistance on the brakes and at a speed of 25 miles per hour. A second run of 20 minutes with a Horse Power at the drawbar of 500 was also made, and no further sign of heating was apparent. Tests were then commenced, but after running for only 20 minutes the R.H. coupling rod bush was again hot. As we had no further new bush for this particular rod end, the rod was sent to the Paris Orleans Works for the bush to be re-metalled and re-bored. The question arose as to the disturbances of the wheel centres by fitting the new driving boxes. Trammels were obtained from the works and the centres were checked both by our own people and by the works testing plant staffs. The rod was returned to the engine at 4.30 p.m. but owing to the number of blow holes in the metal it was rejected.

Thursday December 20

The rod was taken back to the Paris Orleans Works at 7.0 a.m., but they had difficulty in producing a bush in which the white metal was free from blow holes, and it was 7.0 p.m. before commencement was made in refitting it to the engine.

Friday December 21

The engine was placed on the test plant at 8.30 a.m. and ran light throughout the morning. During the afternoon a series of tests at 80, 100, and 120 Kilometres per hour, with 12% cut off were made. Between each test the engine was run light for 20 minutes. All the bearings both in the rods and in the boxes appeared to be bedding down well.

Saturday December 22

The test was discontinued, and the men returned to England for Christmas.

Monday December 31

Staff returned to France.

1935

Tuesday January 1

In view of the uneven beat, the Paris representatives of the 'Dabeg' Company visited the engine to see the valve chests opened up. They suggested that the valves should be set to the crank angles rather than to the valve openings, and the following is a series of readings taken in this manner :-

	Theoretical Figure	Left Cylinder		Centre		Right Cylinder	
		F	B	F	B	F	B
Pre-admission	0°	2.5°	2°	1°	1.5°	3°	2°
Cut off	120°	123°	122°	121°	120°		
Release	154°	149°	155°	153°	154°	133°	151v
Compression	67°	64°	68°	69°	68°	69°	69°

At the request of the 'Dabeg' people also two of the steam valves were reground. All the valve seatings were in good condition and secure within the cylinder casting. All the spring caps on both steam and exhaust valves were fitted when the valve covers were replaced.

Wednesday January 2

The engine was ready to go on the plant at 8.0 a.m. but as the French 'Est" engine had been on test during our absence for the Christmas it was necessary to reset the brakes and rollers of the plant to suit our wheelbase, and it was 10 o'clock before we were able to commence. A preliminary run was made for 15 minutes after which the engine was put on test at 18% cut off and at a speed of 100 Kilometres per hour. The engine ran for 20 minutes to bring the conditions constant when the vertical shaft rotated by our L.H. trailing crank pin, and carrying the motion of the engine up to the dynamometer table, twisted off and the test had to be stopped and the engine returned to the Shed at 12.0 mid-day. During the Christmas break the back plate of the ashpan had been removed. It made no difference, however, to the amount of smoke emitted from the chimney top and opportunity was now taken, while the plant was under repair to change the blast pipe tops to 5.5" diameter with the largest set of vee bars.

Thursday January 3

The engine went on to the plant at 8.30 a.m. and commenced the first test at 9.25 a.m. The first series of test carried out were at 60 Kilometres per hour and at 12%, 18%. 25%, 35% cut off. The second series were at 12% cut off and at speeds of 80, 100 and 120 Kilometres per hour. With the smaller blast pipe the smoke at the chimney was much reduced, but the amount of coal thrown out at the chimney was excessive. At the conclusion of the tests there were signs of the heating up of the L.H. leading axlebox and on removal of the tray there was a considerable amount of white metal round the pad. A pilot driver was obtained and the engine was taken into the Paris Orleans works.

Friday January 4

While the leading wheels were being dropped and the boxes dismantled, the cam boxes were dismantled and opened up for examination. Considerable wear had taken place on the exhaust cams of the R.H. cylinder. The remaining cams and rollers were all in good condition.

Saturday January 5

The work at the Paris Orleans works progressed satisfactorily throughout the day and at 9.0 p.m. the wheels had been replaced under the engine and the running gear etc. refitted. The roller of the R.H. exhaust valve proved to be so badly worn that it was necessary to grind off 2 millimetres in diameter in order to regain it concentricity. The pin of this roller was also worn, and before refitting this cam box it was decided to await the arrival of spare pints and rollers from England. The 'Dabeg' people recommended bronze pins in line with Continental practise, and they put in hand a full set of bronze pins for future fitting if necessary. The left hand cam box was replaced and the valve setting again checked by the 'Dabeg' representatives. The valve spindles were also ground to give them an extra .001 clearance in their housing.

Sunday January 6

The spare rollers and pins were not immediately released by the Customs officials, and were therefore not available. The right hand cam box was reassembled and the necessary adjustment made to the valve spindles to accommodate the reground roller. The blast pipe tops were changed to 5 ¾" diameter with the smallest of the vee bars. The engine was lighted up in the shop and was able to leave the works at 1.0 p.m. It was placed on the plant at 2.30 p.m. and ran throughout the afternoon at 400 Horse Power and from 25 to 30 miles per hour. The beat at the chimney top is still imperfect and is being further investigated by the 'Dabeg' people.

Monday January 7

The engine was placed on the plant at 9.0 a.m. and after a period of running at 400 Horse Power test, conditions were commenced at 12% and 18% cut off at 60 Kilometres per hour. At the end of the tests the left leading box again shewed signs of heating up. The pad was withdrawn and there was a slight trace of metal on the pad. The pad was thoroughly cleaned, new oil supplied, and the engine run light for the remainder of the day. The engine was run light on the plant, but as the L.H. box was running rather warm the engine was taken to the shed for examination.

Tuesday January 8

The whole of the pads, with the exception of those in the driving boxes, were withdrawn. The L.H. intermediate pad and tray contained a considerable deposit of white metal and it was decided to take the engine into Paris Orleans works and fit a remetalled box. There was some delay in the arrival of the pilot driver, and the work of stripping down was not commenced until 4.40 in the afternoon.

Wednesday January 9

The wheels were replaced under the engine and it returned to the testing plant at 7.30 p.m. It was the intention to run the engine on the plant the same evening, but owing to a failure of one of the roller bearings of the plant brake we had to wait until the morning.

Thursday January 10

The engine was on the plant at 8.0 a.m. and commenced running in half hourly periods at 18% cut off and at 25 miles per hour. During the morning it was inspected by a number of visitors, Members of the Committee of Scientific and Industrial Research, and it was kept running until mid-day, the maximum speed being 60 miles per hour. This was the first occasion on which the French oil had been used in the axlebox lubricator, and there appeared to be no signs of heating. The engine came off the plant at 2.30 p.m. to enable the brakes to be reset for the French 'Est" engine which is being put on the plant tomorrow for comparison and for the benefit of the visitors.

Friday January 11

Engine No 2001 was standing aside while the 'Est" engine was under test and opportunity was taken to make a number of small adjustments. The firebars were lifted to enable the ashpan wing plates to be freed from ashes, and the element ends to be cleaned. The performance of the 'Est" engine is very good and the following is a specimen set of figures taken while the test was in progress:-

Cut off	30% High Pressure Cylinder 60% Low Pressure Cylinder
Speed	80 Kilometres per hour (49.7 mph)
Drawbar Horse Power	1600
Pressure in Boiler	19.7 Hectopieze (282 Psi)
Saturated side of Header	19.5 Hectopieze (279 Psi)
Superheated side of Header	18.8 Hectopieze (269.5 Psi)
Superheater Temperature	370°C in the Header (698°F)
Superheater Temperature	365°C in the Steam Chest (689°F)
Smokebox Temperature	350°C at the large Flues (662°F)
Smokebox Temperature	380°C at the small Flues (716°F)
Smokebox Vacuum	105 m/m of water (4.133")
Temperature in L.P. Exhaust	100° (212°F)
Temperature in Firebox	1310° (2422°F)
Temperature entrance to combustion chamber.	1200° (2191°F)
Temperature near Firebox Tubeplate	1060° (1972°F)

Saturday January 12

During the morning we commenced tests at 12% cut off and at 60, 80, and 100 Kilometres per hour. At the end of the 80 Kilometres per hour test everything appeared to be in order and running well, but after 12 minutes at 100 Kilometres the leading axlebox was again hot. It was now suggested by the Paris Orleans engineers that the principle cause of the heating was to be found in the brass bars containing our oil grooves bearing hard on the journal and thus setting up local heating, and it was now decided that the remetalled box which we should fit on the L.H. leading wheel should have a complete white metal bearing in accordance with the French practise. The 'Est" engineers also gave us the adjustments they had found necessary to take up their wedges when running on the plant and our wedges were next set to give these clearances which are as follows:-

Leading wheel	.024 inches
Driving wheel	.008 inches
Intermediate wheel	.024 inches
Trailing wheel	0.32 inches

Sunday January 13

The work fitting the remetalled box to the L.H. leading wheel and the re-erection of the running gear was completed and the engine returned to the plant at 7.30p.m. The blast pipe tops were again altered to 6 inches diameter with the No.1 vee bars.

Monday 14 January

In order to give the remetalled boxes as good a chance as possible the engine was run with a little load (up to 500 Horse Power) throughout the day. There were no signs of heating.

Tuesday January 15
Tests were now made with the new blast pipe at a speed of 60 Kilometres per hour and at 12%, 18% and 25% cut off. Everything was in order and the engine returned to the shed at 4.30 p.m.

Wednesday January 16
In the morning the tests were carried out at 60 Kilometres per hour and 12% cut off, but before the test was completed the L.H. intermediate box failed. It was now decided to take out all the coupled wheels and to remetal the boxes with a complete white metal bearing. It was also decided to burnish the journals. The engine was taken into the Vitry shops at 6.0 p.m. ready to commence dismantling the wheels early the following morning.

Thursday January 17
The first pair of wheels to be dropped was the intermediate pair. Mr Murphy, of Messrs. J. Stone and Company arrived in the evening and went out to the works of Messrs. Corpet Louvet & Company to examine the methods employed in metalling the boxes.

Friday January 18
The wheel lathe in the Paris Orleans shops at Vitry was quite unsuitable for burnishing up our journals. The nearest suitable lathe was that in the new wheel shop of the Nord railway at Ermont, and arrangements were made for each pair of wheels to be taken there by motor lorry for the journals to be turned and burnished.

Saturday January 19
The first pair of wheels were returned to Vitry from Ermont and the first boxes from Messrs. Corpet, but the metalling was not good, especially of the left hand box, and they were rejected.

Sunday January 20
The Paris Orleans works were closed down for Sunday. The metalling of the boxes proceeding at Messrs. Corpet's works, who were now pouring the metal with a 2 inch head above the face of the box. This appeared to be giving good results, and two boxes were sent over to Vitry to commence bedding on the journal the following morning.

Monday January 21 to Friday January 25
The work of taking down the wheels and boxes and of re-erecting proceeded. The outstanding detail was the development of a flake in the R.H. side driving journal during the process of burnishing. This flake was triangular in the shape as indicated:

And it was necessary to turn off the journal at .8mm before the effect of this flake was totally eliminated. After being dealt with at Ermont the diameters of the journals were as follows:-

	Diameter of journals after turning	
Pair of Wheels	**Right**	**Left**
Leading	239.8 – 9.4410	239.8 – 9.4410
Driving	239.2 – 9.4172	240.2 – 9.4566
Intermediate	240 – 9.4488	240.5 – 9.4685
Trailing	240.6 – 9.4724	240.7 – 9.4763
Nominal Size	241.3 – 9.5 ins.	241.3 – 9.5 ins.

The driving journals were finished turned, polished and lapped; the other journals were turned and burnished with a Krupp three roller burnisher.

Messrs. Wakefield Paris office staff thoroughly inspected and tested the lubrication system, and went into the question of providing an oil guaranteed to maintain its viscosity at higher temperatures then the L.N.E.R. express engine oil. The following table gives the characteristics of the oil they supplied, and for comparison the same figures of L.N.E.R., Est, and P.O. oils:-

Oil	Viscosity Redwood seconds at:		
	70°F	140°F	200°F
L.N.E.R No.1 Winter	1500	175	-
L.N.E.R No.1 Summer	1675	195	-
L.N.E.R No 2 Winter	1775	177	-
L.N.E.R No 2 Summer	2100	195	-
P.O.	1550	172	64
Est	3229	209	65
Wakefield's Castrol	2200	247	81

The superiority of this Castrol at 140°F is very marked without being too viscous at 70°F to siphon freely though a pad. This oil was used during the remainder of the tests. The engine returned to the plant on Friday evening, January 25

Saturday January 26
The engine left the shed at Vitry testing plant for a run on the Paris Orleans line. We left Vitry at 7.30 a.m. and except for slacks for stations and curves, maintained a fairly constant speed of 25 miles per hour. We stopped at Juviay and Bretigny to examine the boxes, and arrived at Etampes at 9.25 a.m. a distance from Vitry of 60 Kilometres. There was neither turntable large enough to accommodate the engine at Etampes , nor triangle, and it was therefore necessary to return to Vitry tender first. This was a good test for the engine, as we had eliminated the front oil grooves on the boxes, so the principle source of lubrication when running backwards would be the pad. We stopped at Bretigny and Ivry, and arrived back at Vitry at mid-day. The whole of the boxes were cool. It was intended that the engine should go on the plant in the afternoon, but owing to failure of a brake roller bearing on the plant, we were not able to do so.

Sunday January 27
The boiler was washed out, tube blown out, side firebars lifted, and element ends cleaned in preparation for starting consumption tests on Monday.

Monday January 28
Owing to re-setting of the changed rollers of the plant, it was not possible to start until 10.50 a.m. when an hour's run was made with little load for the purposes of further running in the boxes. They appeared to be bedding down well, and everything was cold. It was also noticed that with the changed rollers the engine rode on the plant much better, and the moving over of the wheels was not nearly so pronounced. In the afternoon the first consumption tests were commenced at 60 Kilometres per hour and at 12% cut off. Excessive movement of the R.H. driving box in the horns was noticed when the engine was running, and it was therefore kept under observation. After 10 minutes it appeared to settle down to a normal movement, but at the end of 20 minutes it bound in the horn and he test was stopped. There was considerable metal in the tray, and the engine went into the Paris Orleans shops at 5.15p.m.

Tuesday January 29 and Wednesday January 30
A remetalled box was fitted to the R.H. driving wheel, and arrangements were made for the engine to go to Tours so that the engine could be lifted and checked over and could be thoroughly run in on the Paris Orleans line.

Thursday January 31

The engine was worked down to Tours, arriving at 5.30p.m. where it was taken into the shops. All the bearings were entirely cold, and in view of this and the way the engine had run, it was felt undesirable to lift it. Arrangements were made for a fast run up to Orleans next day to see if any heating took place under first running conditions. French coal was to be used whilst running over the Paris-Orleans railway.

Friday February 1

The engine ran two double trips between Tours and Orleans, a distance of 72 miles in each direction. Each single journey was carried out Non-stop, the average speeds being as follows:-

Morning	Tours to Orleans	53.328 miles per hour
	Orleans to Tours	61.68 miles per hour
Afternoon	Tours to Orleans	64.44 miles per hour
	Orleans to Tours	63.48 miles per hour

The maximum speed was 82.8 mph. All the bearings ran cold and the engine was in good condition.

Saturday February 2

One similar run to those carried out the previous day was made between Tours and Orleans and back. The bearings ran cold, and arrangements were made to carry out a series of brake engine trials the following week. As the engine had been so long in France a revised and shortened programme of test to be carried out at Vitry were submitted to and approved by Mr Gresley. The programme was as follows:-

No. of Test	Nature of test	Speed Kph	Horse Power	Feed by	Cut off	Reg
1	Consumption	90	750	Pump		
2	Consumption	90	1500	Pump		
3	Consumption	90	2250	Pump		
4	Consumption	90	1500	Injector		
5	Maximum Power	90	-	Injector	35	F

The cut off and regulator opening in tests 1, 2, 3 and 4 were left to the driver's discretion.

Sunday February 3

The boiler was washed out at Tours, and the engine generally prepared for the brake engine tests.

Monday February 4

The engine was weighed, and the necessary adjustment made. The engine then ran a brake engine test run from St. Pierre des Corps to Orleans with the Paris Orleans dynamometer car and three Paris Orleans brake engines. The booked average speed was 70 Kilometres per hour, the cut off 18%, and the regulator full open. The average speed was 65.9 km. an hour, and the average Horse Power 1253. All bearings were cold.

Tuesday February 5

A similar brake engine trial to the previous day was carried out from Orleans to St. Pierre des Corps at an average booked speed of 90 Kilometres per hour, and at 25% cut off. The average Horse Power was 1640, and the average speed was 82 kph. The engine again ran cold.

Wednesday February 6

A third brake engine trial was made between St. Pierre des Corps and Orleans at a booked speed of 110 Kilometres per hour, and at 35% cut off. The average speed was 80.7 kph and the average Horse Power 1910. The engine again ran cold. These three trials were successful as regards the way the engine behaved. It was impossible, however, to maintain the boiler pressure. The French enginemen considered our firehole and door too small, especially for high rates of combustion. They also thought our fire shovel too small, involving the fireman in unnecessary labour.

Thursday February 7
The engine worked back to Vitry leaving St. Pierre at 10.12 a.m., and arrived at the test plant shed at 2.30 p.m. again cold in all bearings.

Friday February 8
The engine was brought to the plant at 9.0 a.m. and the whole of the morning was occupied in resetting the rollers to our wheelbase. The revised programme of tests was taken in hand. The first test was commenced at 2.30 p.m. at 90 Kilometres per hour with a Horse Power of 750. The cut off and steam chest pressure selected by the driver to maintain these conditions were 18% and 125 lbs per sq. inch respectively. The engine ran the full two hours test satisfactorily in every way. At the end of the test the regulator was fully opened for a short time, when it was found that at 90 Kilometres per hour 1600 Horse Power was developed.

Saturday February 9
A test at 90 Kilometres and at 1600 Horse Power was commenced, but the steam pressure could not be maintained. Various methods of firing were tried without any better results. There was much clinker in the fire, and the test was stopped and the engine returned to the shed at 1.30 p.m.

Sunday February 10
The boiler, which was rather dirty, was washed out, tubes blown through, firebars lifted for cleaning out the ashpan wing plates and element ends cleaned. There was a considerable accumulation of 'birdnesting" on the small tubes at the firebox end and several of the large tubes were badly blocked at the element ends, explaining the failure of the engine to steam properly. The blast pipe was changed to 6 inches diameter with the No.3 vee bars, as too much smoke was being made and a sharper blast was required for the higher horse powers.

Monday February 11
The 1600 Horse Power tests were again commenced at 90 Kilometres per hour. The A.C.F.I. installation was not working satisfactory, and was losing too much water out of the heater through the de-oiler valve. Full steam pressure could not be maintained despite the larger vee bars, and although the test lasted 1 hour and 51 minutes, the average Horse Power was only 118- instead of 1600. There was also considerable trouble with the slipping of the wheels on the rollers, especially at the leading coupled wheels, the rollers under which, at intervals, almost ceased to revolve. The effect of this slipping appeared to make the leading wheels oscillate laterally, as the thrust of coupling rods moved over from side to side. The R.D. box ran slightly warm and the engine was stopped to allow it to call down. After the mid-day break the R.D. box ran cold, and it was decided to repeat the 90 Kilometres per hour and 1600 Horse Power test. The engine, however, again developed a tendency for the wheels to move over towards the right, and excessive vibration, especially at the leading and driving wheels, was set up. After the test had run for 27 minutes the L.H. leading axlebox again ran hot. It was decided that this should be the last test and the engine went into the Paris Orleans shops in preparation for its return to England.

Tuesday February 12 and Wednesday February 13
The work of refitting the remetalled box proceeded at the Paris Orleans works while the whole of our material was being collected together and packed into the L.N.E.R. box wagon and the engine returned to the test plant to be coaled and prepared for its journey to La Chapelle.

Thursday February 14
Final arrangements were now being made for the engine to be exhibited at Gare du Nord in Paris, and it left Vitry together with the three coal wagons, box wagon and brake van for the Nord shops at La Chapelle at 10.30 a.m. On arrival at Villeneuve St. Georges, two coal wagons containing about 80 tons of coal were detached as Mr. Vallantin had agreed to take over this coal in order to carry out a trial on the P.L.M. Railway. The engine and the remaining wagons then left Villeneuve for la Chapelle via Le Bourget, arriving in the Nord shops at 4.30 p.m.

ABOVE No 2001 was
tested at Vitry-sur-Seine,
France, between
December 1934 and
February 1935. Gresley's
technical assistant, Oliver
Bulleid, was in charge
of the locomotive.
Ian MacCabe Collection

Friday February 15 and Saturday February 16
The engine was thoroughly cleaned and prepared for exhibition in the Nord was at La Chapelle.

Sunday February 17
At 8.30 a.m. Engine No 2001, together with Mr. Besnerais' saloon, and one of the Nord super Pacifics, were placed for exhibition in no.1 platform of the Nord Station. The exhibition opened to the public at 11.30 a.m. and until 7.0 p.m. there was a continual steam of visitors. During the afternoon one of the 'Maybach' diesel-electric streamlined trains arrived on No 2 platform and this remained on exhibition for the afternoon. The engine was taken back to the shops at La Chapelle.

Wednesday February 20
The engine left La Chapelle at 9.01 a.m. for Calais with its train of three empty 40-ton wagons, 10-ton covered goods wagon, and brake van, via Montdidier, Amiens and Etaples, arriving at 4.10 p.m.

Thursday February 21
The Customs formalities were completed and the engine and stock loaded onto the Train Ferry in the early afternoon. The ferry left for Harwich that evening.

APPENDIX 5

The following extract is taken from the July 1926 Working Timetable and details instructions for the operation of P1 Class locomotives.

Following trains are worked by Mikado engines and convey 100 wagons between New England and London.

UP
328 (9.25 a.m. New England to Ferme Park).
Monday to Saturdays inclusive.

DOWN
116 (5.30 a.m. Ferme Park to New England).
Tuesdays to Saturdays inclusive.
70 (5.0 a.m. Ferme Park to New England
Sundays
Approximate length of trains is 670 yards. Must be worked in both directions with 20 ton brake.

UP
Trains should not pass on to Up Main line at either Westward or Spital Junctions until they can be dealt with by Crescent Junction.
In the event of the Up Home signals at Connington being at danger, drivers must draw well up to them before bringing their trains to a stand, so as to clear safety catch 701 yards north of Up Home signals.
Trains must be run on Up Goods line Connington to Abbots Rippon or Leys; Huntington North No.1 to Offord or beyond, and Arslesey to Cambridge Junction. They must also run on Up Slow or Goods lines Hitchin South to Knebworth or Woolmer Green.
Engines take water at Cambridge Junction.
No.5 Reception Road at Ferme Park to be cleared in readiness.

DOWN
Trains to leave Ferme Park with equivalent of 20 or more empties next engine which must be detached Fletton Junction for use in Brick Yards, except in case of 70 down, Sundays, when wagons must be detached at Holme.
Water to be taken at Biggleswade and the trains must be run on the Goods line from Arlesey. If absolutely necessary for water to be taken at Hitchen drivers must give two crows at Langley, where the signalman must pass the information forward to Stevenage North and Hitchin South, and trains must be turned Slow line from Stevenage.
Engine of 70 down (Sundays) to take water at Hitcin.

IF NECESSARY TO DIVERT MIKADO ENGINE FROM ITS BOOKED WORKING (116 DOWN 5.30 A.M. EX FERME PARK), YARDMASTER AT FERME PARK MUST ARRANGE FOR TRAIN WORKED BY MIKADO ENGINE TO BE MADE UP TO 100 EMPTY WAGONS, AND RUN AS '100 WAGON SPECIAL'.
SPECIAL TO BE TELEGRAPHED FOREWARD '100 WAGON SPECIAL' AND INSTRUCTIONS SHOW ABOVE APPLY. STAFF TO BE PREPARED TO DEAL WITH TRAIN ACCORDINGLY.

BIBLIOGRAPHY

Books

Ahrons, E.L. *The British Steam Railway Locomotive. From 1825 – 1925.* 1927.

Armstrong, Jim. *LNER Locomotive Development.* 1974.

Bellwood, J & Jenkinson, D *Gresley and Stanier.* 1976.

Borge, Jacques *Les Locomotives a Vapeur* 1976

Brown, F.A.S. *Nigel Gresley Locomotive Engineer.* 1962

Bulleid, H.A.V. *Master Builders of Steam.* 1970.

Bulleid, H.A.V. *Bulleid of the Southern.* 1977.

Coster, Peter *The Book of the A1 and A2 Pacifics* 2007

Day-Lewis, Sean. *Bulleid. Last Giant of Steam.* 1964.

Haresnape, Briand. *Railway Liveries 1923-1947.* 1989.

Harris, Michael. *LNER Carriages.* 1994.

Hughes, Geoffrey. *The Gresley Influence,* 1983.

Hughes, Geoffrey. *LNER.* 1986.

Hughes, Geoffrey. *Sir Nigel Gresley. The Engineer and his Family.* 2001.

Jones, Kevin. *Steam Locomotive Development.* 1969.

Knox, Harry. *Haymarket Motive Power Depot, Edinburgh 1842-2010.* 2011.

Morrison, Gavin. *The Power of the A2s.* 2004.

Mullay, A.J. *Streamlined Steam. Britain's 1930s Luxury Expresses.* 1994.

Nock, O.S. *British Locomotive of the 20 Century. Volume 1 1900-1930.* 1983.

Nock, O.S. *The British Steam Railway Locomotive 1925 – 1965.* 1986.

Nock, O.S. *The Locomotives of Sir Nigel Gresley* 1945 (1991 edition)

Nock, O.S. *The Gresley Pacifics* 1982

Peel, Dave. *Locomotive Testing on Britain's Railways 1901-1968. A non-technical overview.* 2013.

Poultney, Edward Cecil. *British Express Locomotive Development 1896 -1948.* 1052.

Proceedings of the Institute of Mechanical Engineers *Locomotives I Have Known*

Proceedings of the Institute of Mechanical Engineers *Test Plant on the Great Western Railway at Swindon*

Proceedings of the Institute of Mechanical Engineers *Address by the President (Gresley)*

Proceedings of the Institute of Mechanical Engineers *Locomotive Experimental Stations*

Proceedings of the Institute of Mechanical Engineers *The Three Cylinder High Pressure Locomotive*

Proceedings of the Institute of Mechanical Engineers *Feed Water Heaters for Locomotives*

RCTS *Locomotive of the LNER . Part 2A. Tender Engines – Classes A1 – A10.* 1978.

RCTS *Locomotive of the LNER . Part 6B. Tender Engines – Classes O1 – P2.* 1983.

Robertson, Kevin. *Bulleid. Man, Myth and Machines.* 2010.

Rodgers, Colonel H.C.B. *Chapelon: Genius of French Steam.* 1972.

Rodgers, Colonel H.C.B. *Express Steam Locomotive Development in Great Britain & France.* 1990.

Stephenson, Brian. *LNER Album.* Volume One. 1970.

Stephenson, Brian. *LNER Album.* Volume Two. 1970.

The Gresley Society. *The P2s. A Photographic Special Edition.* 2013

Tuplin W.A. *The Steam Locomotive.* 1974.

Tuffrey, Peter *Cock o' the North Gresley's Bold Experiment* 2014.

Yeadon, Willie *Yeadons Register of LNER Locomotives. Volume Three. Raven, Thompson & Peppercorn Pacifics.* 2001.

Yeadon, Willie *Yeadons Register of LNER Locomotives. Volume Nine. Gresley 8-Coupled Engines. Classes O1, O2, P1, P2 & U1.* 1995.

Yeadon, Willie *Yeadons Register of LNER Locomotives Appendix Two Locomotive Tender Numbering* 2005

Magazines, Newspapers and Journals

Backtrack. *LNER Locomotive Naming Practise.* January 2001.

Backtrack. *Eight Coupled Express Locomotives.* December 2006.

Backtrack. *Gresley's Mighty 'Mikados'.* January 2014.

Journal of the Institution of Locomotive Engineers *Poppet Valves on Locomotives*

Journal of the Institution of Locomotive Engineers *A New Locomotive Distribution Gear Using Poppet Valves (Caprotti)*

Journal of the Institution of Locomotive Engineers *Modern Locomotive Superheating - Part 1*

Journal of the Institution of Locomotive Engineers *Modern Locomotive Superheating - Part 2*

Journal of the Institution of Locomotive Engineers *Inaugural Address (Gresley)*

Journal of the Institution of Locomotive Engineers *Presidential Address (Gresley)*

Journal of the Institution of Locomotive Engineers *Presidential Address (Gresley)*

Journal of the Institution of Locomotive Engineers *A New Infinitely Variable Poppet Valve Gear*

Journal of the Institution of Locomotive Engineers *The Locomotive Blast Pipe and Chimney Part 2.*

Journal of the Institution of Locomotive Engineers *Locomotive Testing Plants.*

Journal of the Institution of Locomotive Engineers *Poppet Valve Gear as Applied to Locomotives*

Journal of the Institution of Locomotive Engineers

The Counter Pressure Brake Method of Testing Locomotives
Journal of the Institution of Locomotive Engineers
  The Development of LNER Locomotive Design
Journal of the Institution of Locomotive Engineers *2-8-2
  Type express Passenger Locomotive*
Journal of the Institution of Locomotive Engineers
  The Proportions of Locomotive Boilers
LNER Magazine *The 'Cock o' the North' in France.* January
  1935
LNER Magazine *Advertising Notes.* January 1935
LNER Magazine *Three Generations of L.N.E.R Locomotives.*
  January 1935
Railway Wonders of the World. Part 13. *'Cock o' the North'*.
  April 1935.
Railway World. *P2 Potential and A4 Performance.* December
  1972.
Railway World. *I Helped to Build Mons Meg.* November 1982.
Railways. *Locomotive Causerie.* May 1947.
Steam World. *Magnificent 'Mikados'*. January 2013.
Stephenson Locomotive Society Journal. *The Class A.2
  Conversion from P.2".* June 1943
Stephenson Locomotive Society Journal. *The P2 Class 2-8-2
  Locomotives. March 1945*
Stephenson Locomotive Society Journal. *From 'Cock o' the
  North" to 'Saint Johnstoun". August 1968.*
The Gresley Observer. *Various letters and issues.* 1970-2015.
The Locomotive. *Recent Continental Development of the Lentz
  Poppet Valve Gear.* Various issues 1934-1935.
The Locomotive. *Three-Cyl. 2-8-2 Express Loco. L.&N.E.
  Railway.* June 1934
The Locomotive. *Test Run with Engine No 2001 'Cock o' the
  North," L.&N.E.R., between King's Cross & Barkston.* July 1934.
The Locomotive. *2-8-2 Three-Cylinder Engine Lord President.
  L.&N.E. Railway.* July 1936
The Locomotive. *Pacific Locomotive with Poppet Valves, P.L.M.
  Railway.* October 1936.
The Meccano Magazine. *A Test Run on "Cock o' the North"*
  1934
The Railway Engineer. *2-6-0 Type Mixed Traffic Locomotives.*
  May 1932.

The Railway Engineer. *The Manufacture of Monobloc
  Cylinders for 3-Cylinder Locomotives.* September 1932
The Railway Engineer. *Cock o' the North.* August 1934.
The Railway Magazine. *Britain's First Eight-Coupled Express
  Engine. July 1934.*
The Railway Magazine, *British Locomotive Practise and
  Performance.* August 1934.
The Railway Magazine. *Three Generations of Locomotive
  History.* March *1935.*
The Railway Magazine. *British Locomotive Practise and
  Performance.* April 1935.
The Railway Magazine. L.N.E.R. *2-8-2 Express Passenger
  Locomotive 'Cock o' the North" in France. April 1935*
The Railway Magazine, *British Locomotive Practise and
  Performance. July 1935*
The Railway Magazine. *L.N.E.R. 2-8- Locomotive 'Earl
  Marischal". July 1935.*
The Railway Magazine. *On test at Vitry. July 1935.*
Trains Illustrated. *The Gresley Mikados.* September 1956.
Trains Illustrated. *Memories of the Mikados.* September 1956.
Vintage LNER. *Various Issues.*

Other Historical Sources
Cine film of *Cock o' the North* at Vitry held by the P2SLC
  Collection.
Cine film of *Earl Marischal* at York held by the P2SLC
  Collection.
Cine film of *Earl Marischal* leaving Dundee held by the
  P2SLC Collection.
LNER Board minutes held at Public Records Office, Kew.
LNER Traffic Committee held at Public Records Office, Kew.
LNER Locomotive Committee held at Public Records Office,
  Kew.
Correspondence and other written material about the P2
  class held at the National Railway Museum.
Drawings for P2 Class held at National Railway Museum,
  York.
Material relating to Lentz valve gear held at Worcestershire
  Records Office.

INDEX

Aberdeen 8-11, 22-23, 42,45,50-54, 70-73, 78-79, 81-85, 89-91, 96, 98
'Aberdonian' 10, 40, 50, 61, 71, 82
ACFI feedwater heater 27, 34-37, 48, 54, 80
Alfol lagging 37
Amiens 64-65, 68
Associated Locomotive Equipment Ltd 27, 101

Barkston 42, 43, 45, 48
Boilers 15, 21, 25-27, 34-39, 43, 45, 49, 53, 55-56, 67, 71-72, 77-78, 89, 94, 98, 101, 103
Boosters 12-21
Boy scouts 79
Bugatti 75

CAD 99, 100, 103, 105
Calais 63, 64, 68-69
Cams 28-29, 30-31, 34, 51, 63, 73, 97, 101
Camshaft 29-31
Canadian Pacific Railway 37
Cartazzi 13, 14, 24
Chime whistle 37, 43
City & Guilds Engineering College 36, 56
Combustion chamber 77-78, 101
Conjugated valve gear 12-13, 54, 86-88
Cowlairs 77, 85, 90, 92
Crank axle failure 84-85, 88, 100
Crosby Valve and Engineering Company 37

Darlington Locomotive Works 96
Davey Paxman & Company 28, 29, 62
Derailments 83, 84, 88, 100
Doncaster 11-12, 19-27, 34-35, 38-40, 48-49, 51, 53, 55-56, 60, 62-64, 68, 70, 74, 76-77, 79-81, 83, 85, 88-91, 94-95, 98-99, 105
Double chimney 35, 54, 77
Double heading 10
Dundee 46, 50-53, 61, 70-71, 73, 76-83, 85, 91
Dynamometer 16, 18, 43, 45, 48-50, 63, 65-67

Edinburgh 9-10, 22-23, 42, 50-53, 70-73, 75-77, 79-85, 88-89, 90-91, 96
Exhibitions 18-19, 23, 42, 46, 47, 52, 68, 90

Ferme Park 16, 18

Film – Cock o' The North 46-47
Fish trains 81-82, 91
Forth Bridge 8, 53, 72-73
Franklin Railway Supply Company 101

Gill Sans 40
Gordon of Fochabers 79
Gorton 26-27
Great Northern Railway 8, 11, 13, 21-22, 86
Gresley Society Trust 103

Harwich 63, 68
Heenan & Froude 64

In Town Tonight 43, 45
Indicator shelter 45, 48-49, 62

King's Cross 10, 20, 37, 39-40, 42-49, 55-56, 59-60, 62-63, 82, 77, 84, 91
Kirkcaldy 72-73, 84
Kylchap 32, 50, 54

Lentz valve gear 27-31, 54, 62-63, 101
Livery 16, 37, 39, 85, 89-90, 97
LNER Advertising Department 46-47, 79
LNER Operating Department 18, 22, 81, 83, 85
Locomotives:
    A1 (Gresley) 10, 12-16, 21, 34
    A1 (Peppercorn) 78, 94, 96-99, 101-102
    A2 89, 91, 92, 94
    A2/1 91, 94, 98
    A2/2 89, 91-92, 94, 96
    A2/3 94
    A3 10, 15, 21-22, 24-26, 33-34, 36, 38, 42, 44, 49, 54, 56, 73, 79, 83-84, 92, 94, 98
    A4 26, 35, 37-38, 73-79, 91
    B12 28-29, 34
    B12/3 42
    B17 38, 42, 75
    B2 21
    C1 13, 20
    C7 31, 34
    C10 10
    C11 10
    D49 29-30, 33
    Garratt locomotives 16, 40
    Great Northern 11
    J20 28

O1 12
O2 12, 13
P1 12-21, 23
Prince of Wales 7, 97-99, 101-105
SR 'River' tanks 24
Tornado 7, 96-103, 105
V2 26, 36, 88, 91, 94, 99-100
W1 ('Hush Hush') 35, 38-39, 54, 75, 88
London & North Western Railway 11
London, Midland & Scottish Railway 10, 23, 83, 89

Maid of Glamis 79
Monobloc castings 25-29, 54

Names 79, 98
New York Central Railroad 13
North British Railway 8-9, 81
North Briton 94
North Eastern Railway 8, 86
Numbering 12, 16, 39, 90, 96

Oscillating valve gear 28-30

Paris Gare du Nord 68-69
Personalities:
    Allen, C. J. 56, 58, 60
    Arbuthnott, G. 70, 73, 81
    Boulby, J. 34, 63
    Broughton 27-28
    Bulleid, O. V. S. 21-24, 27-29, 38-39, 43, 51, 63, 65-67, 78, 80-81, 86
    Campbell, T. 70, 71, 81
    Captain Howey 37-38
    Chapelon, A. 32, 33, 53, 62
    Cox, E.S. 87
    Dalby, Prof. 36, 75
    Gant, W. 63, 66
    Giles, F. 43
    Gill, E. 40
    Godfrey, B. 102-103
    Godfrey, T. 102-103
    Gresley, H. N. G. 10-13, 15-16, 21-25, 28-38, 42, 44-45, 48, 51, 53-54, 56, 62-63, 67, 71, 73-75, 77, 79, 81, 85-88, 91-92, 96-98, 103
    Hardisty, Fireman. 71
    HRH The Prince of Wales 97-98
    Ingersoll, H. 13
    Ivatt, H 13, 22-23

Ivatt, M. 22
May, J. 102-104
McGuire, D. 50, 52
Nock, O. S. 70-73
Parker, L. 76
Peachy, C. 45
Peppercorn, A. 78, 86, 88, 92, 94, 96, 98, 102
Sheddon, Driver 71
Sowdon, W. 53
Spencer, B. 24
Stanier, W. 73, 87, 89
Thom, R. 24, 26, 28, 39, 40-41, 64
Thompson, E. 21, 78-79, 85-94
Trask, E. 88
Trower, G. 43, 53, 63, 66
Webb, F. W. 11
Windle, E. 40-41, 51, 63, 88
Wintour, F. 22
Peterborough 12, 16, 20, 42-43, 45, 48-49, 55, 58, 94
Piston valves 27-29, 31, 54, 56, 73, 77, 80, 88

Poppet valves 27-32, 62-63, 72, 80

'Queen of Scots' Pullman 94

Railway Magazine, The 56, 79
Romney Hythe & Dymchurch Railway 28, 36-37
Rotary valve gear 29-31, 54, 97, 100-101

Sheds:
 Aberdeen Ferryhill 42, 73, 78, 82, 91
 Dundee Tay Bridge 61, 70, 76-78, 81, 85
 Edinburgh Haymarket 42, 49 50, 70, 73, 76-77, 81-83, 85, 90-91
 Peterborough New England 16, 18, 20, 94
 Doncaster 55
 King's Cross Top Shed 43, 47, 83
 York Shed 94
Sleeper cars 10
Smoke lifting plates 33, 35, 39, 56, 59, 104
Stockton & Darlington Railway Centenary 16, 19
Streamlining 35, 38-39, 45, 56, 68, 74-80,

82, 84, 89-90, 97, 105
Superheaters 10, 12-13, 14, 25-26, 49, 78, 89, 92
Swing link truck 13, 24, 72, 84, 88, 99

Taper blocks 33, 49, 50, 53, 55
Tay Bridge 10, 71
Tenders 14, 16, 21, 38-40, 54, 79, 89, 90, 101-102
Testing 32, 36, 43, 46, 48-50, 53, 55-56, 62-67, 70, 75, 79, 91, 97, 99-100
The Superheater Company 12-14
Tours 66
Train ferry 63, 68

Vitry 49, 62, 64-70
Walschaerts valve gear 29, 32, 54, 56, 77, 80, 88, 101
Welding 23, 38-39, 87
Whistles 37-38, 43, 104
Wind tunnel testing 36, 56, 75

York 29, 54, 91, 94, 97, 99

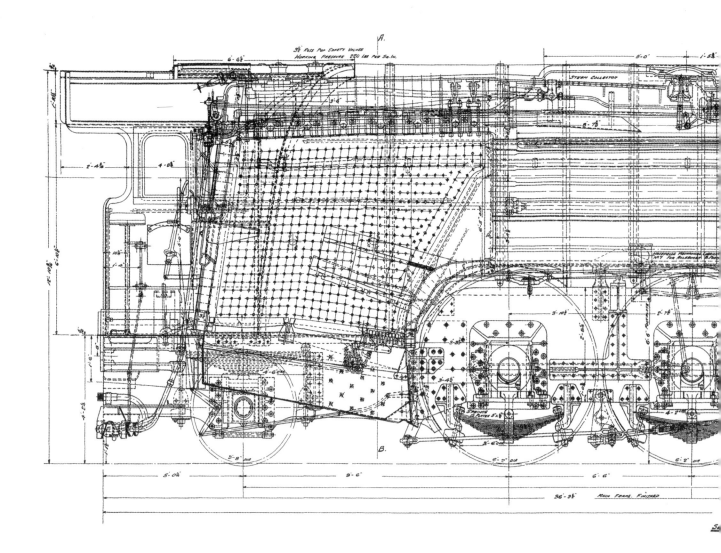

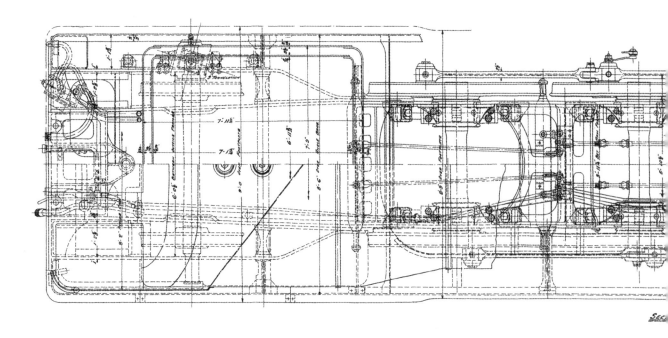

2-8-2 THREE CYLINDE

WHEELS 6'-2" DIAR

SCALE